A
GUIDE
TO
TYPE
DESIGN

A GUIDE TO TYPE DESIGN

Sean Morrison

Prentice-Hall, Inc.
Englewood Cliffs, NJ 07632

Library of Congress Cataloging in Publication Data

MORRISON, SEAN, (date)
    A guide to type design.
    Bibliography: p. 201
    Includes index.
    1. Type and type-founding.   2. Printing, Practical.
I. Title.
Z250.M877 1986   686.2'24   85-11989
ISBN 0-13-371329-6

Editorial/production supervision: Linda Mason and Kim Gueterman
Cover design: Sean Morrison
Manufacturing buyer: Ed O'Dougherty
Page layout: Gail Cocker

This book was designed and illustrated by the author.
The text—11/13 Perpetua—was set on a Linotron 202
The text paper is 50 pound Mead Publishers' Matte.

Printed in the United States of America

10 9 8 7 6 5 4 3 2

ISBN 0-13-371329-6   01

Prentice-Hall International (UK) Limited, *London*
Prentice-Hall of Australia Pty. Limited, *Sydney*
Prentice-Hall Canada Inc., *Toronto*
Prentice-Hall Hispanoamericana, S.A., *Mexico*
Prentice-Hall of India Private Limited, *New Delhi*
Prentice-Hall of Japan, Inc., *Tokyo*
Prentice-Hall of Southeast Asia Pte. Ltd., *Singapore*
Editora Prentice-Hall do Brasil, Ltda., *Rio de Janeiro*
Whitehall Books Limited, *Wellington, New Zealand*

To George Resch and Volney Croswell, two better designers than I shall ever be, from whom—whether they knew it or not—I learned a great deal

CONTENTS

CONTENTS

INTRODUCTION

This text was written in the first place for students of graphic design and typography. However, it is also aimed at a very different reader.

Some time ago, in the course of compiling an article on electronic publishing, I surveyed a number of large corporations to find out where and how they were buying their type. Somewhat to my surprise, they were all setting at least some of it in house. And that started me wondering where they were finding their designers and compositors; there just weren't enough professionals to go around. It turned out that much of the work was being done by designated staff, usually from the public relations or corporate communications division, few of whom had any prior training.

This text, then, is also designed as a reference and handbook for them and their successors—at least until I and my academic colleagues can provide their replacements.

Because of this mixed readership, I have dispensed with the customary end-of-chapter apparatus. In any case, I find that, more often than not, I ignore the printed exercises and produce my own. If you are teaching a design course—clearly you aren't a student, because students never read introductions—you can probably devise more interesting and pertinent practice for your students than I can. And if you are a willy-nilly corporate designer, you certainly have more practical problems to work with.

Obviously, this is not an exhaustive handbook of typography. It deals only with the basics of type design, and I have tried to include enough practical advice and working principles to get you started. I may, in fact, have erred on the side of too many rules-of-thumb, but it seems to me that you can't break the rules successfully—as every good designer does—until you've got them under your thumb. Every seasoned designer knows there is only one rule in typography: If it works, it's right. The problem at the start, however, is knowing what works and what doesn't. There are few things more frustrating for a new practitioner than reinventing square, hexagonal, and elliptical wheels.

The prime emphasis is on text design, for several reasons. First, most of what we read (and consequently most of what we design) is running text. Few of the basic guides on the subject seem to deal with it in depth—largely, I suspect, because display is more variegated and far more exciting. However, if my students are anything to judge by, it is more difficult to produce a readable text design than to create, say, a striking logotype or magazine nameplate. Pure display problems tend to be more tightly focused and the range of solutions much broader. But I am convinced that understanding basic design principles is fundamental to both, although the application of those principles offers a more subtle challenge with text.

Second, this book is too small, in every sense, to deal adequately with display. There is always a temptation in writing a handbook to try and cover everything, which usually means that you deal with nothing satisfactorily. Display tends to be a variegated and fairly specialized field of typography, and many designers, I suspect, gravitate to a specialty after serving a more generalized apprenticeship. This text is designed for the apprentice; there are a number of excellent books on the more specialized branches of design, such as advertising and packaging, for readers who would like to explore further. Finally, I am at heart a book designer, and I see no reason to avoid that bias in my own textbook.

As always, there are a number of people who deserve some small and inadequate recognition for their help; principally Michael Shavelson, director of the Design Center at Boston University's College of Communication; Connie Robichard and Norbert Florendo of Compugraphic Corporation, the latter of whom supplied many of the type specimens in Chapter 3; Ray Pell of Mergenthaler Linotype, who supplied most of the rest; Monika and Julian Brenard, who lent me the word-processor on which the text was produced and tolerated innumerable intrusions on their time and living space while it was being produced; and the many students on whom the material that formed the basis of this text was tested and tempered.

The type samples were set on a Compugraphic MCS 8400. The quotations used in the samples are taken from Bruce Rogers' *Paragraphs On Printing*, published by Dover Publications, Inc., and are used with their permission. The photographic prints for Chapter 1 were furnished by the Pierpont Morgan Library and are reproduced with their permission. The prints of the Linotype machine, the line of matrixes, and the Monotype keyboard and caster in Chapter 4 were loaned by Lloyd Simone Publishing Company; most of the remaining prints of equipment were supplied by the manufacturers. Their cooperation is gratefully acknowledged.

1 FROM GABBLE TO GUTENBERG

Communication is not a human monopoly. Most organisms communicate in one way or another. Humans simply do it more often and with less provocation than other species. We are nature's blabbermouths. But we are unique in one respect. We alone have developed methods of recording and transmitting our messages across time and space.

Perhaps the most ancient of these is writing. Nobody really knows how old writing is; perhaps the earliest example is a series of scratches on a bone dating back about 135,000 years, although the interpretations of the marks have been challenged.

However, by about 20,000 B.C., humans were busy cutting and painting symbols on cave walls, cliffs, rocks, bones and antlers, and, although these early messages may never be completely deciphered, they demonstrate that writing was well established at that point.

The earliest writing systems were pictographic. The symbols stood, literally, for the objects they depicted. This one-to-one correspondence, however, severely limited communication. The writers had to have an enormous inventory of signs to communicate at anything but the simplest level, and the clarity of the message depended to a large extent on the writer's graphic skill. It was also virtually impossible to convey abstract ideas.

Eventually, pictographic systems evolved into more sophisticated ideographic systems that could deal with abstractions. The symbols remained essentially drawings, but they took on abstract as well as literal meanings through the addition of arbitrary signs called determinants. For example, the sun might

I

be represented by a circle surrounded by rays. With a time-determinant, it could take on the additional meaning of "day" or "summer". The symbols also tended to become stylized and standardized so that they were easier to write and to translate.

One of the earliest standardized ideographic systems developed in Mesopotamia by 4,000 B.C. It consisted of clusters of wedge-shaped marks, known as cuneiform, that could be impressed quickly in a soft clay slab with a reed stylus. Another and better known system, hieroglyphics, evolved in the Nile Valley not long after the appearance of cuneiform.

Ideographic writing still required a large number of symbols and considerable graphic skill. Writing became the monopoly of well-trained scribes, who, in Egypt, enjoyed high status. They went through a rigorous training, and apprentices were admitted to the ranks only after they could demonstrate mastery of at least six hundred hieroglyphs.

The next advance was the invention of the syllabary, in which, for the first time, the symbols represented the sounds of speech rather than objects or ideas. The syllabary's major advantage was a radical reduction in the number of symbols needed to write. The signs could be strung together in endless combinations to represent all the words in the language. By the sixth century B.C., the Persians, who had inherited cuneiform from its inventors, had reduced the hundreds of ideographic wedge-clusters to a mere 41 syllabic groups.

Some cultures have never felt the need to go beyond this stage. Chinese script is a mixture of stylized pictograms, ideograms, syllabic signs and determinants that has not changed significantly for many centuries. A reasonably literate Chinese reader must be able to recognize something like 20,000 of these characters. On the other hand, a twentieth-century reader has no difficulty with the most ancient texts. Moreover, groups whose spoken dialects are unintelligible to each other can communicate in writing because they use a common ideographic script. In western society, only numerals have this supercultural capacity. The symbol 5, for example, is pronounced "five" by an American, something like "fïnf" by a German, "sank" by a French speaker, "chinkway" by an Italian, and "penta" by a

Greek, but means the same thing to all five (or finf or chink-way) of them.

In the West, however, the evolution of writing took one further vital step—the invention of the alphabet, whose symbols represent phonemes, the simplest sound-units of speech.

The first alphabets appeared between 1,700 B.C. and 1,500 B.C. along the eastern littoral of the Mediterranean.

Although they varied considerably in appearance, they had one feature in common; they consisted exclusively of consonants. The early Semitic writing resembled our real estate ads—3 rms rvr vw—and became decidedly difficult to translate centuries later.

The Phoenicians, who were a mercantile culture, exported their alphabet along with their trade goods around the Inland Sea. The Greeks acquired it about 1,000 B.C. and refined it over the next six centuries into a 24-letter system, now with vowel signs. The Athenian version was passed on to the Romans, who gave it essentially the form we use today. (The Greeks, however, retained their original alphabet and a variant of it is used in the USSR. The Hebrew, Arabic and Persian alphabets evolved separately.)

The original Latin alphabet lacked the letters J, U and W, which were added later to represent sounds used in non-Latin languages.

The alphabet used throughout most western cultures crystallized at that point, as far as the basic structure of the letters is concerned. However, the letterforms have continued to evolve, particularly in type, where thousands of variations of the theme have been created over the centuries.

The Romans themselves had three distinct written alphabets.

The most formal was called *capitalis quadrata*—square capitals—or *capitalis elegans*—elegant capitals. This form is probably the oldest, and may originally have developed as a stonecutter's alphabet. The letter-forms certainly owe more to the chisel than to the stylus or pen. On the other hand, we know from abandoned trial pieces that the carved inscriptions were first laid out with a brush. Whatever the fact, square capitals were generally reserved for stone monuments and formal documents.

SQVARECAPITALS ELEGANTBVTHARD

Capitalis rustica, or rustic capitals, were used for less formal purposes. This script was narrower, more compact and flowing than the complex square capitals. The letters took fewer strokes to make and used up less space on expensive parchment or papyrus.

RUSTICCAPITALSSIMPLER ANDFASTERTOEXECUTE

Rustic capitals became the handwriting of the educated Roman and the standard book script. By the time of the Republic, an army of slaves was kept busy turning out copies of the most recent best-seller. In fact, it would seem that a high percentage of the Roman population could read. Newspapers, in the form of posters, were displayed regularly in the forums of Roman towns, and political slogans and other obscene graffiti were scrawled on the walls of buildings everywhere.

For even more mundane occasions, the Romans used a simplified scrawl called *scriptura cursiva* (running script) or *littera epistolaria* (letter-writing script).

4

Roman. cursive. y. almost.
a. semi. minuscule.

This hand could be dashed off quickly with a reed pen or scratched into a wax tablet with a stylus. It was written so quickly that the letters often became linked together and developed long hooks and tails. Although, like the other Roman scripts, this was a majuscule, or all-capital, alphabet, these odd-sized letters foreshadowed the development of the first minuscules or small letters.

The use of all three scripts spread throughout the Roman Empire, which at one stage stretched from the British Isles to the borders of India. They served a huge conglomerate population, most of whom claimed Roman citizenship, although many of them probably had little idea where Rome was.

Gradually, however, these provincials took over the administration of the empire. They hybridized the Roman culture, and eventually produced their own hybrid script.

By the third century A.D., this new script, uncial, had become the official script of the empire.

uncialsusedse
ueralminiscul
eletterforms

The name is something of a mystery. *Uncia* is the Latin for "one-twelfth" and is the ancestor of "inch" (one-twelfth of a foot) and "ounce" (one-twelfth of the Troy pound). However, uncial script doesn't seem to be one-twelfth of anything.

It was a smaller, rounded script, with letterforms based partly on the cursive alphabet. At the same time, it retained something of the elegance of the rustic capitals. More importantly, it established an alphabet with different-sized letters, and these eventually evolved into the first true miniscule, or lower-case, script, half-uncial, which appeared at about the same time.

halfuncialthe finstruemini sculealphabet

By the fourth or fifth century, these newer scripts had displaced the earlier Roman scripts, and they survived the fall of the Roman Empire. As independent states emerged from the ruins, they began to take on distinctly regional characteristics. By the seventh century, most areas of Europe had their own distinctive variations of the uncial and half-uncial alphabets.

Diversification came to an abrupt halt toward the end of the eighth century. In 789, Charles, son of Pepin III and soon to be crowned Holy Roman Emperor Charlemagne, decreed that only one script was to be used officially throughout his territories. He imported a remarkable English monk, Alcuin of York, to oversee its design. Alcuin was eventually installed as abbot of the monastery of St. Martin at Tours where the new script, Carolingian miniscule, evolved primarily.

Carolingian miniscule: forerunner of the roman type alphabet

Carolingian miniscule was not a completely new invention; it was, rather, a skillful blending of the best features of contemporary and earlier scripts into a graceful, but practical, whole.

Its letters are reduced to the simplest forms, written with the minimum number of strokes. The pen is held at an angle, producing regular variations in the thickness of the strokes, which serve both to differentiate the letters clearly and to improve their legibility. The writer's hand is always held at the same angle, so there is none of the constant shifting and repositioning required by many earlier scripts (as many as four different hand-positions are needed to form some of the square capitals). Carolingian miniscule is remarkable mainly for its combination of clarity, elegance and practicality. It is a working scribe's script that can be written rapidly without losing its style.

Perhaps its most innovative feature was the amalgamation of majuscule and miniscule alphabets; the Carolingian script established the conventions of capitalization that we still follow. It also consolidated the use of punctuation and of consistent word-spaces.

Strangely enough, although Charlemagne seems to have been able to read, he apparently never learned to write his script. (He signed formal documents with an elaborate monogram, but most of it was executed by a scribe, leaving his majesty to fill in just two letters in the center.) But even if he could not write, many of his subjects could and did voluminously. His empire was run by a large, efficient civil service—and where would bureaucrats be without paper?—supported by a reliable postal service that functioned better than many of its successors.

Charlemagne's heirs, however, lacked his political acumen

and breadth of vision. Through a mixture of egomania, greed and bullheaded stupidity, they dismantled his empire, and it deteriorated into a collection of small, separate states. The once-universal Carolingian miniscule, like the Roman scripts before it, began to go through a series of regional transformations, some of which would have been unrecognizable to Alcuin.

The most radical departure was the form that developed in northern Europe, and more particularly in the Germanic states. Here, the generous rounded forms degenerated into a narrow, cramped, spiky script that mirrored the architectural style of the period, with its tall, narrow pointed arches. The more civilized southerners called both "Gothic", which in their terms meant "barbarian".

The church also adopted this Gothic blackletter for liturgical use, despite the fact that, even at its best, it is not notably readable. However, it had some offsetting advantages. Its straight strokes were easier to learn and simpler to write than the more subtle Carolingian script, no small advantage when many of the monk-scribes were barely literate. Its narrow forms could also be crammed economically on expensive parchment sheets. In fact, the ultimate version of the blackletter, a rigidly upright, angular, densely-packed script, came to be known as Textura—woven—because the pages of text resembled tightly woven cloth.

In southern Europe, the regional variants never departed entirely from the Carolingian model.

In Italy especially, closely allied forms survived until the Renaissance, when a new style of script, patterned directly after the

A typical example of fifteenth-century German Textura blackletter script.

8

℟. Iste est iohannes qui sup
pectus dni in cena recubuit bea
tus apostolus cui reuelata sut
secreta celestia. ℣. Valde hono
randus est beatus iohannes.
℟. Qui supra pectus dni in ce
na recubuit. ORATIO.

Ecclesiam tuam qs
domine benign
illustra: ut beati iohis
apostoli et euuangeliste
illuminata doctrinis
ad dona perueniat sem
piterna. per dominum.

Sequencia sancti euuan
gelii secundum lucam.

In illo tpe Missus
est angelus gabri
el a deo in ciuitate
galylee cui nomen na
zareth ad uirginem des
ponsatam uiro cui no
men erat ioseph de do

mo dauid. et nomen
uirginis maria. Et i
gressus angelus ad e
am: dirit. Aue gracia
plena dns tecu benedi
cta tu in mulieribus.
Que cum audisset tur
bata est in sermone e
et cogitabat qualis es
set ista salutacio. Et
ait angelus ei. Ne ti
meas maria: muen
sti enim graciam apd
dnm. Ecce concipies i
utero et paries filium
et uocabis nome eius
ihm. Hic erit magnus
et filius altissimi uo
cabitur. Et dabit illi
dns deus sedem dauid
patris eius. et regna
bit in domo iacob in e
ternu. et regni eius no

Sic etiam in stabulo semper sic cenat in agro
Non fit ergo aliud non habet immo suum

M·VAL·MARTIALIS
EPIGRAMATON·LIB·VII·

AD CAESAREM·

CCIPE BEL
LIGERAE
CRVDVM
THORACA
MINERVAE

Ipsa medusee quem timet ira dee
Dum uacat hec cesar poterit lorica uocari
Pectore cum sacro sederit egis erit
Inuia sarmaticis domini lorica sagittis
Et martis getico tergore fida magis
Quam uel adethole securam cuspidis ictu
Texuit innumeri lubricus ungus apri
Felix sorte tua sacrum cu tangere pectus
Fas erit & nostri mente calere dei
I comes & magnos illesa merere triumphos
· Palmateq, ducem sed cito redde toge
AD PONTILIANVM.

Carolingian, was adopted. It is known as humanistic, or roman, cursive.

The scholars of the Renaissance selected this script deliberately. In the first place, it was more elegant than the surviving regional hands, and more consonant with the reviving interest in the arts. It also contrasted sharply with the Gothic scripts of the barbarian north, and it came to symbolize the humanists' rejection of its reactionary feudalism and the narrow clericalism of the Church.

However, they also seem to have assumed that the Carolingian miniscule was the authentic script of the classical authors whose works were the foundation of Renaissance scholarship and the humanist philosophy. In actuality, few original Latin or Greek texts had survived. The versions known to the fifteenth century were mostly copies made by Carolingian scribes in a conscious effort to preserve the classical literature.

Whatever the reasons, the roman cursive became the standard book-hand of the Renaissance and its use eventually spread throughout most of Europe. At the same time, a narrower, slanted and more economical version developed for official documents. It was known as *cancellaresca corsiva*—chancery cursive—or italic script.

The roman and italic hands became the immediate models for the first typefaces in Italy, and eventually for the type alphabet that predominated in the West, except for Germany. And this despite the fact that printing was perfected in Germany.

The origins of printing are almost as obscure as the origins of writing, and for much the same reason—its inventors never used their new medium to record the process.

Nevertheless, by the ninth century, the Chinese were printing from wooden blocks, although their use seems to have been confined at first to printing prayer scrolls. By the eleventh century, they had progressed as far as movable types of fired clay and metal. However, at that point, the movement stalled, partly for want of a suitable ink. The water-soluble inks used for writing and block printing were neither dense nor viscous enough for printing from metal type.

A page of roman cursive written by Bartolomeo Sanvito or one of his disciples about 1480. From a copy of Martial's Epigrammata *commissioned by the Gonzaga family.*

11

S'extenderanno anchor tutte le lingue;

Et e (come huom ch'extingue

Ogni altra voluptà) fia solo intento

A d'haver cura del commesso armento.

Qual altro hebbe giamai terrestre impero,

Che havesse le virtù simili a questo,

Feroci in guerra, e mansuete in pace?

Non fu il piu giusto mai, ne'l piu modesto,

Ne'l piu giocondo insieme, e'l piu severo,

Ne'l piu prudente anchor ne'l piu verace.

Ogni ben operar tanto li piace,

Che giorno, e notte ad altro mai non pensa.

E però Dio, che sua virtute immensa

Nel principio del mondo antivedette,

Volse l'opre piu elette

A lui serbare; acciò, che'l mondo tutto

Si possa rallegrar di si bel frutto.

Dunque Signor, poi che ne l'alto seggio

Per vicario di Dio seder ti truovi,

Et hai la cura de la gente humana,

Muovi'l profondo tuo consiglio, muovi,

E da la scabbia ria, ch'ognihor fa peggio,

The Koreans persisted, however, and by the thirteenth century had perfected the casting of metal type in sand molds. They attempted to re-export the process to China and Japan, but without success. The complexity of Oriental scripts, in which hundreds of symbols must be combined into thousands of configurations, made printing impractical. The complex forms could be cut more economically in wood, even though the resulting blocks could not be used for anything but their original purpose. In any case, the Chinese and Japanese cultures preferred to reproduce their revered classical literature in its original form, so there was little incentive to switch from calligraphy to type. Calligraphy was also among the most highly regarded arts; print, by its very nature, lacked the unique, personal touch of the master scribe.

Consequently, type was never fully deployed in the East, and printing was largely relegated to mundane tasks such as the reproduction of playing cards and paper money, a combination that, at one stage, touched off a wave of inflation that almost toppled the Chinese empire.

These block-printed playing cards and bills were already familiar in Europe by the fifteenth century, but apparently nothing was known about printing from movable type. The process had to be rediscovered from the start.

Certainly, by the fifteenth century, the conditions were ripe. All the essential materials and equipment were in place. The craft of papermaking, another Chinese discovery that had reached Eruope through the Arabs, was well developed. Punch-making, a critical process in type manufacture, was highly sophisticated in such activities as gold- and silver-smithing. Metal-casting was also a mature business, and had reached a level of perfection in the minting of coins and medals. Presses were used in a variety of trades—weaponsmithing, cheese- and wine-making, textile processing—and the Van Eycks, a family of Dutch painters, had recently introduced the technique of painting with an oil medium, a suitable vehicle for printing ink.

By the early part of the century, the Dutch were printing books from movable type, a development that has been credited

Cancellaresca corsiva or italic script written by Vicentino Arrighi, one of the foremost Italian calligraphers of the Renaissance.

13

to Laurens Costers of Haarlem. However, the perfection of the process must be attributed to the genius of Johann Gensfleisch zur Laden, better known by his adopted name, Gutenberg.

It has been suggested that Gutenberg's only invention was the adjustable type mold (the earlier Dutch types had been cast in individual molds, making the business impossibly cumbersome). This alone would have been a significant achievement. But there is no serious doubt that Gutenberg took an infant technology and raised it to maturity in an unbelievably short span of time.

Exactly how he did it remains a mystery. Very little is known about his life. Our major sources are the official records of a seemingly endless series of legal imbroglios in which he was involved, many of them provoked by his unwillingness or inability to pay his debts.

Gutenberg was born in Mainz sometime just before 1400, and may have been illegitimate, since he adopted the name of his mother's birthplace. He was trained as a goldsmith—an ideal groundwork for his later activities—and joined the local goldsmith's guild. However, the craftsmen's guilds in the city became embroiled in a bitter dispute with the powers-that-were, and, in 1430, Gutenberg decamped to Strasbourg, where he went back into business with several partners. The evidence in a later lawsuit by the heirs of one of these partners reveals that he also began to develop his printing equipment in the strictest secrecy. Exactly what he was doing is not clear, and we will probably never know more about this critical period in his life.

In 1448, however, he returned to Mainz with his—apparently—perfected system, because he was able to borrow 800 guilders from a local financier, Johann Fust, using his equipment as security. Two years later, Fust injected an additional 800 guilders in the business as the price of a partnership, and to bail out what was beginning to look like a failure. Gutenberg seems to have been something of a perfectionist, and Fust was becoming impatient at the lack of progress.

Gutenberg was probably working on his masterpiece, the so-called Mazarin 42-line Bible. How far he had progressed is not clear, but, in 1455, Fust sued Gutenberg for the return of his

A page from Gutenberg's 42-line Bible, printed on vellum.

de hebreis voluminibus additu noue
rit eque usqz ad duo pucta iuxta theo
dotionis dumtaxat editione: qui sim
plicitate sermonis a septuaginta inter
pretibus no discordat. Hec ego et uo
bis et studioso cuiqz fecisse me sciens
no ambigo multos fore qui uel inui
dia uel supercilio malent contemnere
et uidere predara quam discere: et de
turbulento magis riuo quam de pu
rissimo fore potare. Explicit prologus
Incipit lib' psalmor' vl' soliloquorum.

Beatus uir qui no
abijt in consilio im
piorum: et in uia pec
catorum no stetit:
et in cathedra pesti
lentie no sedit. Sed
in lege domini uolutas eius: et in lege
eius meditabit die ac nocte. Et erit
tamqz lignu quod platatum est secus
decursus aquaru: qd fructu suu dabit
in tpe suo. Et foliu eius no defluet: et
omnia quecuqz faciet prosperabutur.
Non sic impij no sic: sed tamqz pul
uis que proicit uentus a facie terre.
Ideo no resurgut impij i iudicio: neqz
peccatores in consilio iustoru. Quoni
am nouit dominus uia iustor: et iter
impiorum peribit. Psalmus dauid

Quare fremuerut getes: et populi me
ditati sunt inania? Astiterut
reges terre et principes conuenerut in
unu: aduersus dum et aduersus cristu ei.
Dirumpam' uincla eor: et piciam'
a nobis iugu ipor. Qui habitat ce
lis irridebit eos: et dns sublanabit eos.
Tunc loquet ad eos in ira sua: et in
furore suo coturbabit eos. Ego au
tem costitut' sum rex ab eo super syon
montem sanctu ei': predicas preceptu
eius. Dominus dixit ad me filius

meus es tu: ego hodie genui te. Po
stula a me et dabo tibi gentes heredi
tatem tua: et possessione tua finibus
terre. Reges eos i uirga ferrea: et tam
qz uas figuli confringes eos. Et nunc
reges intelligite: erudimini q iudica
tis terra. Seruite dno i timore: et ex
ultate ei cu tremore. Apprehendite di
sciplinam: ne quado irascatur domi
nus et pereatis de uia iusta. Cum ex
arserit in breui ira eius: beati omnes
qui confidunt in eo. Psalmus dauid
cu fugeret a facie absalon filij sui

Domine qd multiplicati sunt qui
tribulat me? multi insurgut ad
uersum me. Multi dicut anime mee:
no est salus ipsi in deo eius. Tu aut
dne susceptor me' es: gloria mea et ex
altas caput meu. Voce mea ad do
minu clamaui: et exaudiuit me de mo
te sacto suo. Ego dormiui et soporat'
sum: et exsurrexi quia dns suscepit me.
Non timebo milia populi circudan
tis me: exurge dne saluu me fac deus
meus. Quoniam tu percussisti omnes
aduersantes michi sine causa: dentes
peccatoru contriuisti. Domini est sal':
et super populu tuum benedictio tua.
In finem i carminibus psalmus dauid

Cum inuocarem exaudiuit me deus
iusticie mee: i tribulatione dila
tasti michi. Miserere mei: et exaudi o
ratione mea. Filij hominu usqz quo
graui corde: ut quid diligitis uanita
tem et queritis mendacium? Et scitote
quonia mirificauit dns sanctum suu:
dns exaudiet me cu clamauero ad eu.
Irascemini et nolite peccare: qui di
citis in cordibus uestris, in cubilibus
uestris compungimini. Sacrificate
sacrificiu iusticie et sperate in domino:
multi dicunt qs ostendit nobis bona.

loans with interest and was awarded the press and printing equipment in settlement. He proceeded to take over the business with Gutenberg's most skilled worker, Peter Schoeffer, who eventually, like many before and since, married the boss's daughter. Fust and Schoeffer published the Bible.

Somehow or other, Gutenberg was still in the printing business in Mainz two years later, and was still operating in 1466 when he retired on a pension from a local bishop. He died two years later.

Gutenberg's types were indistinguishable in design from the blackletter scripts of the period. He even reproduced many of the contractions and abbreviations used by the scribes to save time. He set a pattern, however, that was to be followed by German type designers for the next five hundred years.

As the craft of printing spread, other and more influential type alphabets came into use. And the craft spread remarkably quickly. By the end of the fifteenth century, presses were operating in every major city in Europe. More than a thousand printers were in business, and had turned out something on the order of two million books. The first transatlantic press was established in Mexico City less than a generation after Columbus sailed for the New World.

Many of these early printers were Germans who escaped from Mainz when the city was sacked in 1462 during a minor war between two local bishops. In that year, two of the refugees, Arnold Pannartz and Conrad Sweynheym, who may have learned his trade in Gutenberg's shop, set up the first press in Italy, at a monastery in Subiaco near Rome. Their early typefaces might be described as semi-Gothic or semi-roman.

They retained the essentially spiky character of the Italian blackletter script, but had obviously been influenced by the rounder humanistic script of Italy.

The first purely roman type was designed by another exile, Nicolas Jenson, who set up his press in Venice about six years later.

Jenson had been master of the royal French mint at Tours. In

A page from Sweynheym and Pannartz' edition of St. Augustine's De Civitate Dei, *published in 1467.*

Voniam cōstat oīm rerum optandarum plenitudinē esse felicitatē: quę nō ē dea sed donū dei: et ideo nullū deū colendum esse ab hoībus: ñ q pōt eos facere felices. Vnde si illa dea eēt: sola colenda merito diceret. Iam consequēter uideam9: qua cā deus qui pōt & illa bona dare quę haberi possunt eñā nō boni ac per hoc etiam nō felices: romanū impiū tam magnū tanq̃ diuturnū esse uoluerit. Quia .n. hoc deoȝ floȝ illa quā colebāt multitudo non fecit: et multa iam diximu9: et ubi uisum fuerit oportunū esse dicemu9. Causa g magnitudínis imperii romani nec fortuita ēst nec fatalis: ſm eorū sniam siue opionem q ea dicūt esse fortuita: quę uel nullas cās hñt uel nō ex aliquo rōnabli ordie ueientes: et ea fatalia quę pręter dei & hoīum uolūtatē cuiusdā ordis necessitate cōtingūt. Prorsus diuīa puidētia rgna cōstituūt hūana. Quę si ꝑptere a qſq̃ fato tribuit: quia ipam dei uoluntatē uel ptātem fati noīe appellat: sentēciam teneat: linguam corrigat. Cur .n. nō hoc pmū dicat quod postea dictur9est: cū ab illo qſq̃ quęsierit quid dixerit fati: Nam id hoīes quādo audiūt usitata loquēdi consuetudíne: nō intelligūt ñ uim posinois siderū: qualis ē qñ qs nascit siue concipit. qd aliq alienāt a dei uolūtate: aliqui ex illa eñā hęc pendere cōfirmāt. Sed illi q sine dei uolūtate decernere opīnanē sidera qd agamu9: uel quid bonoȝ hēamu9maloruue patiamur: ab auribu9oium repellendi sunt. Nō solū eoȝ q ueram religionē tenēt: ſȝ qui deoȝ qualiūcunq̃ licet floȝ uolūt esse cultores. Hęc eñ opio qd agit aliud nisi ut nullus oīno colat aut rogetur dñs. Contra quos

contra eos qui pro defensione eoȝ quos deos putant xanę religiōi aduersantur. Illi uero q positioni stellarū quodāmodo decernentiū qualis qſq̃ sit: et qd̃ pueniat bōi quidue mali accidat ex dei uolūtate suspendunt: si easdem stellas putant hēre hāc ptātem traditam sibi a summa illius ptāte ut uolentes ista decernant: magnā cęlo faciūt iniuriā: ī cui9uelut clarissimo senatu ac splendidissima curia opīnātur scelera facienda decerni: qualia si aliqua terrena ciuitas decreuisset: generi hūano decernēte fuerat euertēda. Quale deínde iudiciū de hoīm factis deo relinqē: qbus cęlestis necessitas adhibēt: cū dñs ille sit et siderū & hoīm? Aut si nō dicūt stellas accepta qdez ptāte a summo deo arbitrio suo ista decernere: ſȝ ī talibu9necessitanbu9 ī gerendis illius oīo iussa cōplere: ita ne de ipo senciendum est: qd̃ indignissimum uisum est de stellarum uolūtate sentire? Quod si dicunt stellę significare poti9ista q̃ facere: ut q̃ locutio quędā sit illa posīo pdicens futura nō agēs: nō .n. mediocer doctoȝe hoīm fuit ista sentencia. nō q dem ita solēt loqui mathematici: ut uerbi gra dicant: Mars ita positus homicidā significat ſȝ homicidam nō facit. Verūtamē ut cōcedamu9nō eos ut debet loqui: et a phis accipet oportere sermoïs regulam: ad ea prenūcianda quę ī siderū posīone repire se putant: qd sit de quo nihil unq̃ dicere potuerūt: cur ī uita gemmoȝ: ī actioibu9 et ī euentis: ī professionibus: artibus: honoribus: ceterisq̃ rebu9ad hūanā uitaȝ ptinētibus: atq̃ ī ipa morte sit plerunq̃ tanta diuersitas: ut similiores eis sīt q̃ tii ad hęc actinet multi extranei: q̃ ipi inter se gemíni p exiguo temporis interuallo ī nascēdo separati: ī cōceptu aūt p unū concubitū uno eñā momento semīnati.

Icero dicit Ipocratem Ca. scdm nobilissimū medicū ſcptū reliqſse:

1458, so the story goes, his master, Charles VII, sent him to Mainz to study printing. It is not clear why he never returned to France. One, perhaps apocryphal, explanation is that he was not at all popular with Charles' successor, the infamous Louis XI, and decided that it would be wiser to move on to Italy. Whatever the reason, by 1468 he was producing unique typefaces derived directly from the roman script.

Jenson's roman typefaces became the model for most type designers after him. However, there still remained one major development in the evolution of the type alphabet.

About 1500, Aldus Manutius, a leading Italian scholar/printer, commissioned one of the first independent typefounders, Francesco Griffo, to design a new type for a series of pocket-sized editions of the classics—the forerunners of the modern paperback. Jenson's broad roman faces were too extravagant with paper; Aldus needed something more economical.

Griffo turned to a fairly obvious model, the tight-fitting italic script, and designed the first italic typeface, which Aldus used to print a Virgil and a Juvenal in 1501.

Jenson's romans and Griffo's italic established the basic pattern of the type alphabet. Countless designers have created innumerable variations on it in the intervening five centuries. And, in that sense, the alphabet has continued to evolve.

With the advent of printing, however, the evolution has taken a new direction.

We know virtually nothing about the inventors of the script alphabets; even Alcuin's role in the development of Carolingian miniscule is obscure and disputed. In fact, there is no evidence that any script was the product of a single individual, invented deliberately.

Typefaces, on the other hand, are consciously created artifacts. We know who designed most of them, and many are actually named after their designers. As a result, the type alphabets are extremely varied and highly individual.

At the same time, typefaces are proprietary products, designed to meet the demands of the market. Significant changes

Jenson's influential roman type first appeared in this edition of Eusebius, published in 1470. Aldus Manutius acquired Jenson's punches, matrixes and types after his death in 1481.

ERVM Quoniam hoc uolumen satis iam creuit ad duodecimum librum transgressi quæ restant ad ostédendam platonicam philosophiam ab hebræis defluxisse coscribemus: ut multi uideant nō nobis solū: uerum etiā Platoni iampridem scripturam hebræorū placuisse. *C i Quod querere legibus non querere rationem Iuuenes debent*

Enset igit sine dubitatione aliqua leges sequédas esse hoc modo scribés in primo de legibus. Si quis recte laconum aut cretensiū leges reprehendere possit aliqua quæstio est. Ego autem iudico optimā esse legé: quæ iubet ne quis iuuenū cogitari. Senex autē si qs dubitauerit principibus aut æqualibus referat nemine iuuenū audiente. Non ne igitur multo ante Platonem diuinæ litteræ fidem cæteris proposuere uirtutibus. Vnde apud nos quoqʒ icipiétibus ac iperfectionibus quasi secundum animum infantibus simplicius scripturæ legūtur. Credédū enim omnibus est omnia quæ in ea feruntur sicuti dei uerba uerissima esse. Illis autem qui ad maiorem iam habitum scripturarum puenerūt altiora petere: ac rationem singulorum quærere conceditur: hos iudæi quasi scripturarum expositores secundarios appellare solebant: poetā deinde Plato ait Theognim ex megara Siciliæ testem habemus: qui ait fidelem uirum omni argento atqʒ auro in seditione meliorem. Nemo enī integer atqʒ fidelis sine omni uirtutis numero in seditionibus esse potest. Quorsum hæc? quia legis latorem qui a Ioue missus é ita leges conscribere oportere césemus ut ad maximam semp uirtutū respiciat: quam theognim secuti fidem quæ maxime in periculis luc& esse arbitramur: eam non iniuria perfectam iustitiam nominare possumus. Ita Plato non irrationalé fidem: sed eam quæ uirtuti coniūcta é cóprobare uidetur: quod Saluator noster breuius aptius ac diuinius posuit. Euge inquit serue bone atqʒ fidelis. Et rursus: quis ergo erit fidelis & prudés paterfamilias: prudentiam enim & magnanimitatem fidei coniunxit. Præterea Plato aliquantulum progressus. Certe inquit defunctorum animæ uirtutem quandam habent: qua uel post mortem rebus humanis auxiliantur. Vera enim hæc opinio est: sed nisi prolixis rationibus probari nō potest. Credere autē oportet huiusmodi sermoibus: quoniā a priscis ualde uiris traditi sunt. Credendum ergo est etiam illis: qui ita hæc se habere legibus confirmant. Sic certe de Hieremia traditum fuisse iudæi contendunt. Et machabæorum liber rettulit uisum ipsum fuisse post mortem orare pro populo.

C ii Qʒ cōmode p fabulas adolescentibʒ maiora tradenda sunt

AENE·

E recta, ingenti tedis, atq; iliæ secta,
I ntendítq; locum sertis, et fronde coronat
F unerea, super exuuias, ensém'q; relictum,
E ffigiem'q; toro locat haud ignara futuri.
S tant aræ circum, et crines effusa sacerdos
T er centum tonat ore deos, Herebúm'q;, Chaos'q;,
T er geminám'q; Hecaten·tria Virginis ora Dianæ.
S parserat et latices simulatos fontis Auerni,
F alcibus et meßæ ad lunam quæruntur ahenis
P ubentes herbæ nigri cum lacte ueneni,
Q uæritur et nascentis equi de fronte reuulsus,
E t matri præreptus amor·
I psa mola, manibus'q; piis altaria iuxta
V num exuta pedem uinclis in ueste recincta
T estatur moritura deos, et conscia fati
S ydera, tum si quod non æquo fœdere amantes
C uræ numen habet, iustúm'q;, memór'q; precatur.
N ox erat, et placidum carpebant fessa soporem
C orpora per terras, syluæ'q;, et sæua quierant
A equora, cum medio uoluuntur sydera lapsu,
C um tacet omnis ager, pecudes, pictæ'q; uolucres,
Q uæ'q; lacus late liquidos, quæq; aspera dumis
R ura tenent, somno positæ sub nocte silenti
L enibant curas, et corda oblita laborum·
A t non infelix animi Phœnißa, nec unquam
S oluitur in somnos, oculis ue, aut pectore noctem
A ccipit, ingeminant curæ, rursús'q; resurgens
S æuit amor, magnó'q; irarum fluctuat æstu·
S ic adeo insistit, secúmq; ita corde uolutat,
E n quid agam? rursus' ne proccos irrisa priores
Experia

in their design are usually occasioned by equally significant changes in the applications of type. Written alphabets also changed with shifts in societies and cultures, but the rate of change was slower and the change itself less clearly motivated.

Consequently, typefaces mirror more immediately and precisely the periods in which they were designed, and chart the progressive changes explicitly. And, unlike the script alphabets which flourished, declined and disappeared, they survive and persist. Many, in fact, are resurrected after a period of disuse to take on a new lease of life and carry the flavor of their time to a later generation of readers. The type alphabets form a permanent and continuing record of the societies they have served over a half-millenium, and will probably continue to play the same role as long as print survives.

The diversity of the huge inventory of typefaces, each with its own unique personality, is one of the major challenges facing the type designer. We will grapple with that problem in a later chapter.

Griffo's italic type was designed specifically for this edition of Virgil's works, published by Aldus Manutius in 1501.

2 TYPE TALK

People have been predicting the demise of print for years, but the gloomy forecasts, like Mark Twain's obituary, seem to have been premature. Print not only survives, but perversely flourishes in the electronic era; print revenues have risen at an average of 5 percent annually since the 1950s. Ironically, one of the largest producers of printed products is the computer industry, and the highest-circulation magazine in the United States is *TV Guide*. In fact, more people than ever before are becoming entangled with type as computerization makes typesetting simpler and more accessible.

Print is ceasing to be the domain of the specialist. Many large corporations, once merely purchasers, now have in-house typesetting equipment and are producing their own materials on a large scale. At the opposite end of the spectrum, small retail businesses and community organizations are becoming directly involved in print communication, and recent industry forecasts predict a steady decline in the number of commercial typesetters and printers, perhaps by as much as 20 percent over the next decade.

However, the entry of nonspecialists into the field has created some novel hazards. Many of these newcomers wander into type territory with little training, and often with no idea of how to communicate with the natives. Unhappily, Berlitz has not yet added a crash course in Conversational Typography to its curriculum although the language of type is as arcane as Tibetan or Turkestani to most people. It has evolved over five hundred years and originated with a typesetting technology that is now practically obsolete.

If you have to deal with type and type people, you need a basic vocabulary, and it will seem less like gibberish if you know something about its origins.

OVERTURE AND BEGINNERS

The production of metal type started with the making of a punch. This was a slightly tapered steel stake cut off square at the narrower end. The punch cutter, who was in effect the designer, sketched the letter or symbol in reverse on this flat surface and carved it out in relief with files. However, if there was an enclosed area, such as the inside of an O, another punch, called the counter-punch, was made to this shape and driven into the flat end of the master punch, leaving a slight indentation. The outside form of the letter was then cut around it. We still call these blank, enclosed areas **counters**.

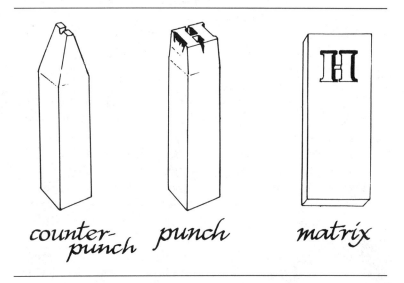

counter-punch *punch* *matrix*

The raised letter-shape was then hammered to a precisely controlled depth in a softer strip of metal, forming the **matrix** which would eventually mold the printing surface of the letter. Any device that creates a printed form is still called a matrix, or **mat** for short, even if it is a film negative or a string of digital bits.

The matrix was clamped into a metal mold, consisting essentially of two interlocking, L-shaped blocks of metal, held together with a strong spring. These could be opened or closed to adjust to the different letter-widths and shaped the **body** or shank of the piece of type with the raised letter, formed by the matrix, on top.

Molten type metal was poured into the mold and allowed to set. The finished piece was then removed and dressed with a file to remove burrs and other imperfections. This small slab of metal is called a **type**, **stamp**, or **character**, the term we use now for any printed letter, numeral or symbol.

The characters were stored in compartmented drawers called **cases**. The cases were removed from the storage cabinet as they were needed and stacked on a frame where the typesetter could reach them easily. By convention, the case of capital letters was always mounted above the case of small letters, and the two sets of characters eventually became known as the **upper case** and the **lower case**.

The printing surface of the type, shown in black on the following page, was called the **face**, the term we now use for an individual design of the type alphabet.

In the early days, printers often designed their own faces, cut

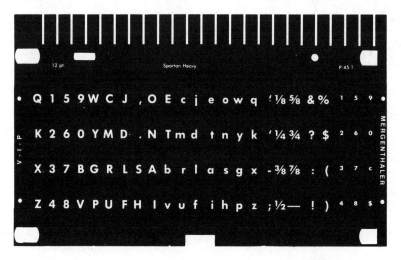

The matrixes for Mergenthaler's VIP phototypesetter are negative images carried on a strip of film.

25

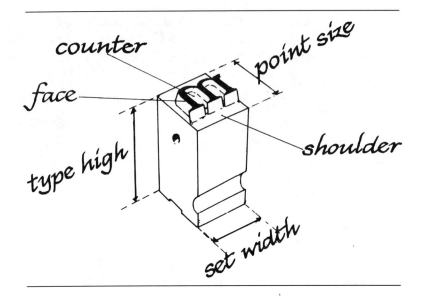

the punches, cast the type, set it, and printed it on paper they had made themselves. Typefaces were not usually interchangeable from one press to another. However, as printing spread, typefounding, typesetting and printing became specialized crafts, and the need for standardization was gradually recognized.

Even so, it was not until 1737 that a standard measurement for type sizes was proposed by Pierre Fournier, a leading French typefounder. He suggested that type sizes be standardized and measured in **points**, or seventy-seconds of the Imperial French inch. The proposal made perfect sense, but it took a royal decree to force French typographers to conform to it; the type industry is nothing if not conservative.

Fournier's scheme was later refined by the Didots, who succeeded Fournier as the leading French typographers, and their version of the point, which measures 0.01438″, was generally adopted in Europe (and, for some obscure reason, Brazil). It is named the Didot after them.

American typesetters did not get around to systematizing type sizes until 1878, when they settled on a point measuring 0.013873″, demonstrating with a single stroke a sturdy spirit of independence and the typographer's taste for peculiar numbers. The British adopted the American point about a decade later.

This is the unit we use now to measure type sizes, rules, and some odd characters such as bullets; spaces between characters; and spaces between lines. It is, to all intents and purposes, still 1/72″ if you are not fussy about a few hundred-thousandths of an inch—and, when it comes to six-digit fractions, I for one am not in the least fussy.

To put it another way, **there are 72 points to the inch**.

The sizes of type have been standardized pretty much everywhere. They range from 3 points to 144 points, although you will rarely run across the smaller and larger sizes. The smallest size in general use is 5.5 point type, which is used mostly for want ads and similar notices in newspapers. It was once the standard size for all ads, and was called **agate**. (Before point sizes came in, type sizes were identified by names; the smaller types were called after gems.) Advertising copy is still measured in agate inches, which you will find marked on designer's rulers.

The type case eventually stored the two sets of characters side-by-side, with the capitals and numerals on the right. The size of the lower-case compartments depends on the number of characters stored, which was dictated by the frequency of use.

Here are the common sizes of type:

5pt It is a truism that almost every face of type has its ideal size, and lessens in merit as this size is either increased or decreased

5½pt It is a truism that almost every face of type has its ideal size, and lessens in merit as this size is either increase

6pt It is a truism that almost every face of type has its ideal size, and lessens in merit as this size is either i

7pt It is a truism that almost every face of type has its ideal size, and lessens in merit as thi

8pt It is a truism that almost every face of type has its ideal size, and lessens inc

9pt It is a truism that almost every face of type has its ideal size, and l

10pt It is a truism that almost every face of type has its ideal si

11pt It is a truism that almost every face of type has its id

12pt It is a truism that almost every face of type has

14pt It is a truism that almost every face of t

16pt It is a truism that almost every fac

18pt It is a truism that almost ever

24pt It is a truism that al

36pt It is a truism

The middle range of sizes (from 9 point to 14 point) are most widely used for running copy, and they are known as **text faces**. The larger sizes are called **display faces**. "Display" is the general term for any kind of type that is intended to be highly visible and eye-catching, and, as we will see later, the principles for designing text and display are quite different.

There is an old saying in typography that up to 14 points we see the words, and over 14 points we see the letters. Like many old typographic saws, this has been validated by more scientific studies.

In the 1890s, it was first established that we do not read letter-by-letter, word-by-word, line-by-line. Instead, our eyes hop along the text in a series of jerky moves, stopping to focus on significant words, and then moving back to fill in the blanks. By the age of about ten, we have acquired a large inventory of word-shapes and our reading pattern has become fixed. However, as type size increases, we find it more difficult to grasp word-shapes as coherent wholes and we resort to piecing the words out letter by letter as we did when we first started to read. It is not entirely clear why this happens, but there is no doubt that over 14 points we are more aware of the letters than the words, and this finding is critical for the type designer.

With the decline of metal type, there is no real reason to hang onto the traditional type sizes. Phototypesetting and digital systems can produce virtually any size of type by manipulating the image optically or electronically.

10pt It has often been said that printing, as well as other arts,

10½ pt It has often been said that printing, as well as other

11 pt It has often been said that printing, as well as other arts,

11½ pt It has often been said that printing, as well as other

12 pt It has often been said that printing, as well as other

12½ pt It has often been said that printing, as well

13 pt It has often been said that printing, as well

13½ pt It has often been said that printing, as

14 pt It has often been said that printing, as

14½ pt It has often been said that printing,

15 pt It has often been said that printing,

15½ pt It has often been said that printing,

16 pt It has often been said that print

Nevertheless, we still use them and probably will for some time to come.

A second standard unit of measurement in type is the **pica. A pica equals 12 points or**—approximately—**1/6″**. Picas are used to specify the length of the type line, or **measure**. They are also used to specify most other measurements in the layout, such as the depth of the text block and margins. In fact, only two things are measured by inches in type design; the **trim size**, or final size, of pages, and the size of illustrations.*

---

* There is growing pressure to metricize type measurements, but so far it has produced no results, even in those countries that have already adopted the metric system.

A designer's rule, with picas along one edge and inches along the other. The back side usually carries agate and inches.

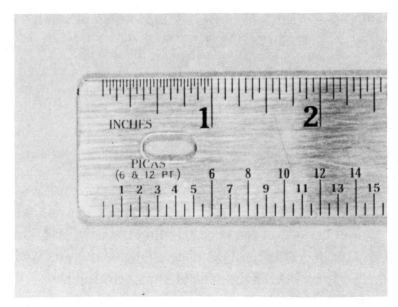

Layout measurements can be given in whole picas, picas and half-picas, or, for irregular fractions, picas and points.

"Pica" is the old name for 12 point type and it is still used for the larger typewriter face. (The smaller face is elite, an old name for 10 point type.) The origin of the name is a mystery. It was the Latin for magpie, a black and white bird related to the crows. In the Middle Ages, it was attached to a clerical rule-book, which, perhaps lacked the colored illuminations typical of other medieval manuscripts. The only other "pica" is the medical term for an overwhelming urge to eat unsuitable substances such as dirt and chalk, but that doesn't seem any more likely as a source than clerical handbooks—or any less, for that matter.

The third unique type measurement is the **em**. Ems are used to specify indention and some forms of spacing. Originally, the em was a blank metal type, lower than the printing types, that was used to fill out short lines. It was square, like the body of the cap M from which it took its name. As a measurement, it is the square of the point size of the type. In 8 point type, the em is 8 points × 8 points; in 36 point type, it is 36 × 36 points; and so on.

There were also multiples of the em, known as **slugs**, and fractions of the em, called **spaces**. Half an em-space was an **en-space**. The smaller fractions are:

30

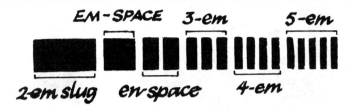

- ☐ 3-to-the-em (1/3 em or thick space)
- ☐ 4-to-the-em (1/4 em or mid-space)
- ☐ 5-to-the-em (1/5 em or thin space)
- ☐ 6-to-the-em (1/6 em or hair space)

Just to make life more difficult, these are usually called 3-em space, 4-em space, and so on, which makes them sound like multiples of the em. However, the key word is "space", which always means a fraction. ("Em" and "en" also sound alike, so they were called "mutton" and "nut" to distinguish them.)

Paragraphs are traditionally indented one em, and you will get a one-em indent automatically if you do not specify something different. Other indentions, such as the indentions before lists, are also specified in ems. Wordspaces used to be specified in fractions of ems, and dashes still are. The parenthetical long dash—like this—is an **em dash**. The shorter dash used to show a range of numbers, e. g., 1980–83, is an **en dash**. The more meticulous typesetters also insert hair spaces before semicolons, colons, question marks and exclamation points and the apostrophes of contractions, such as "don't", to distinguish them from possessives. Hyphens are also preceded and followed by hair spaces.

Ems are another hangover from metal type and are gradually being superseded by a more precise method of spacing—the **unit system**. The system originated with the Monotype Corporation, but is now almost universal in film and digital typesetting. The reference point is the width of the matrix of the cap M. This is divided into 18 units or some multiple of 18. The width of all other characters, and their letter-spacing, is then defined as so many of these units.

In most typefaces, single-stroke characters, such as i, j, and l, are usually 4 units wide; punctuation marks, 5 units; most

The unit system allows for more refined spacing than the em-based system because the unit is directly related to the design of the individual face.

lower-case characters, 9 or 10 units, and most caps, 12 or 13 units. When type is set, the machine counts the number of character units as they are set, compares the running total to the specified number of units in the line, and, as the two approach, adjusts the wordspacing to fill out the line by distributing any leftover units among the wordspaces.

Every character has about a unit of spacing on each side which can be shaved down to fit the letters closely together, permitting very precise letterspacing, which was almost impossible with metal type.

Reducing space is called **minus-spacing** or **kerning**; increasing space is called **plus-spacing**. Here are some examples of incremental minus-spacing:

Letter-spacing is often misused.
Letter-spacing is often misused.
Letter-spacing is often misused.
Letter-spacing is often misused.

The spaces between lines are still specified in points. If no space is added, the type is set **solid**. However, most typefaces look better if the lines are moved farther apart, or **leaded**. In metal type, lead or brass strips were inserted between the lines to increase the space. Hence, the word "leading" and its pronunciation, "ledding". Contemporary typesetting systems space the lines by positioning the type optically on film, so the term leading seems inappropriate. In fact, it is now being replaced by **interlinear spacing**, which is more realistic if a bit wordy. I will use the term **linespacing**, to keep things simple.

The same text set solid and with 1, 2, and 3 points of linespacing. Linespacing can improve the readability of type and alter its appearance dramatically.

It is unfortunate, at least for writers on the subject, that the terminology of printing is largely made up of words that, while almost indispensable in describing its processes, have so many other meanings and implications.

It is unfortunate, at least for writers on the subject, that the terminology of printing is largely made up of words that, while almost indispensable in describing its processes, have so many other meanings and implications.

It is unfortunate, at least for writers on the subject, that the terminology of printing is largely made up of words that, while almost indispensable in describing its processes, have so many other meanings and implications.

It is unfortunate, at least for writers on the subject, that the terminology of printing is largely made up of words that, while almost indispensable in describing its processes, have so many other meanings and implications.

Leads were made in 1 point, 2 point and 3 point thicknesses, and we still tend to specify linespacing in whole points, even though the systems we use now can linespace in fractions of a point. In fact, many of them can minus-linespace—why, I have no idea—by shaving off the small amount of spacing above and below the character on the matrix.

Traditionally, lines of text were set to the same measure, or **justified**, with the first and last characters aligned under one another, or **flush**. Now, however, more designers are setting type with only the left margin flush and the right side of the text uneven, or **ragged right**. One advantage of this format is that the word spaces remain uniform because the typesetter does not have to adjust them to stretch or squeeze lines into a fixed measure.

Type can also be set **ragged left**, with a flush right margin; **centered**, with the lines evenly balanced on the center axis; or **free-form**, without any common point of alignment.

33

Here are the five basic settings.

It is also a mistaken ideal to try to make *all* lines fill the full measure, so as to produce a solid rectangle of type. One doesn't mind a solid rectangle occasionally, when it comes naturally so, but too much of it is monotonous. Many designers tackle the problem as though they were engineers rather than artists.

It is also a mistaken ideal to try to make *all* lines fill the full measure, so as to produce a solid rectangle of type. One doesn't mind a solid rectangle occasionally, when it comes naturally so, but too much of it is monotonous. Many designers tackle the problem as though they were engineers rather than artists.

It is also a mistaken ideal to try to make *all* lines fill the full measure, so as to produce a solid rectangle of type. One doesn't mind a solid rectangle occasionally, when it comes naturally so, but too much of it is monotonous. Many designers tackle the problem as though they were engineers rather than artists.

It is also a mistaken ideal
to try to make *all* lines fill the full measure,
so as to produce
a solid rectangle of type.
One doesn't mind a solid rectangle occasionally,
when it comes naturally so,
but too much of it is monotonous.
Many designers tackle the problem as though they were
engineers rather than artists.

It is also a mistaken ideal
to try to make all the lines fill the full measure,
so as to produce
a solid rectangle of type.
One doesn't mind a solid rectangle occasionally,
when it comes naturally so,
but too much of it is monotonous.
Many designers tackle the problem
as though they were engineers
rather than artists.

The last three settings are not suitable for text because they lack a consistent left margin to anchor the reader's eye. Without a fixed reference point, on which your eye can home in almost mechanically, it is all too easy to miss the beginning of a line. At best, you have to grope around before you find it; at worst, you pick up the wrong line altogether. More often than not, by the time you have found the right place, you have forgotten what the first line said and have to read it again. Reading becomes a chore instead of a smooth, effortless flow.

A typeface is made up of a series of **fonts** in each style and size of the face. Essentially, a font is the set of characters that was stored in a single case. Here is a font of Times Roman:

THE CAST OF CHARACTERS

ABCDEFGHIJKLMNOPQRSTUVWXYZ&
abcdefghijklmnopqrstuvwxyz fifffffiflffl
ABCDEFGHIJKLMNOPQRSTUVWXYZ&
1234567890   [(.,:;!?"-/¢$ — %#*†‡§•.)]   1234567890

To be more precise, this is the 12 point **regular roman** font; "regular" because it is medium weight, and "roman" because the characters are upright. Most roman fonts have companion **italic** fonts, with slanted, more-scriptlike letters. This is the 12 point italic font of Times Roman:

ABCDEFGHIJKLMNOPQRSTUVWXYZ&
abcdefghijklmnopqrstuvwxyz fifffffiflffl
1234567890   [(.,:;!?"-/$ — %)]*

Some typefaces, particularly sans serif faces, have **oblique** or **slanted roman** fonts instead of italics.

These are roman faces tilted over about 12 degrees to the right. A few faces have both italic and oblique roman fonts.

ABCDEFGHIJKLMNOPQRSTUVWXYZ&
abcdefghijklmnopqrstuvwxyz

35

The font has complete upper-and lower-case alphabets, including **ligatures**, or linked letters. Some ligatures are traditional script forms, such as the AE and OE combinations that were common in Anglo-Saxon and Greek, and the ampersand, &, which is a stylized "et", the Latin for "and". Others are holdovers from metal type, and always include an f or ff. The upper arm of the f sometimes hung over the edge of the type and was easily snapped off, so these ligatures were cast on a single piece of type to take care of the problem.

There are two sets of **numerals**. The set on the right are called **modern** or lining figures because they align with the capitals. The set on the left are **old style figures**. They have ascenders and descenders like the lower case. Lining figures are generally used in statistical work because they are uniform in size and easy to read. Old style numerals are generally used for numbers in the text, such as dates, and for page numbers, which are called **folios** by typesetters.

In between are the **punctuation marks**, or **points**, and **reference marks**, such as the asterisk. **Book fonts**, like this, usually have a full set of reference marks; **job fonts**, which are used by general typesetters, have a different, more varied set of symbols.

Times Roman also has a set of **small caps**, which align with the x of the lower case. These were once used for subheads or to set the first line of a major section of text, often after a large decorative initial. They are never found in italic fonts and are rare in the more modern typefaces.

These are the basic components of a font. Some typefaces however, have more elaborate fonts which may include:

$$\ddot{A}\ddot{a}\acute{A}\acute{a}\grave{A}\grave{a}\hat{A}\hat{a}\tilde{A}\tilde{a}\varsigma$$

Accents or **accented characters** for setting foreign languages.

$\frac{1}{4}$ $\frac{1}{2}$ $\frac{3}{4}$ $\frac{1}{8}$ $\frac{3}{8}$ $\frac{5}{8}$ $\frac{7}{8}$ ⅛ ⅜ ⅝ ⅞ ⅓ ⅔ ½ ¼ ¾

Fractions, which come in two versions; **case fractions**, with small numerals set vertically and separated by a bar, and **lining** or **full fractions**, with the numerals separated by a slash. They used to be cast on single types, and were confined to the more common fractions. Odd fractions, known as **piece fractions**, could be built up from superior and inferior numerals separated by an en-dash or slash.

$$+ - \times \div \pm = °'\quad {}^{1234567890}/_{1234567890}$$

Mathematical signs, such as addition and multiplication signs, and **superior** and **inferior** numbers.

To   Ta   Vo   Va   Wo   Wa

Logotypes, which, like ligatures, consist of two characters cast on a single piece of type. Logotypes were designed to overcome awkward letterfits, such as a T followed by a lower-case letter which always produces an unsightly gap because of the large counter under the arm of the T. Digital typesetters are now programmed to kern, or close up, certain letter-pairs automatically, making logotypes superfluous. ('Logotype' is used now almost exclusively for an organizational or corporate symbol. In the era of handset type, it was often a logotype in the original sense; many companies cast their corporate name on a single slug of type because it was often set in an unusual or custom-designed face that the average typesetter would not have in stock.)

A B C D E G J K L M N P Q R T U W Y h k v z

Swash characters, which were decorative alternatives for the regular characters, usually with curlicued serifs.

In addition to the regular and italic fonts, many typefaces also have **boldface** fonts with heavier letterforms, **lightface** fonts with skinnier letterforms, **extended** or **expanded** fonts with characters stretched horizontally, and **condensed** fonts with characters compressed horizontally.

Here are some of the many variants of the typeface Helvetica, which are sometimes called collectively the Helvetica family:

---

abcdefghijklmnopqrstuvwxyz
ABCDEFGHIJKLMNOPQRSTUVWXYZ

abcdefghijklmnopqrstuvwxyz
ABCDEFGHIJKLMNOPQRSTUVWXYZ

abcdefghijklmnopqrstuvwxyz
ABCDEFGHIJKLMNOPQRSTUVWXYZ

abcdefghijklmnopqrstuvwxyz
ABCDEFGHIJKLMNOPQRSTUVWXYZ

abcdefghijklmnopqrstuvwxyz
ABCDEFGHIJKLMNOPQRSTUVWXYZ

abcdefghijklmnopqrstuvwxyz
ABCDEFGHIJKLMNOPQRST

abcdefghijklmnopqrstuvwxyz
ABCDEFGHIJKLMNOPQRST

abcdefghijklmnopqrstuvwxyz
ABCDEFGHIJKLMNOPQRSTUVWXYZ

abcdefghijklmnopqrstuvwxyz
ABCDEFGHIJKLMNOPQRSTUVWXYZ

abcdefghijklmnopqrstuvwxyz
ABCDEFGHIJKLMNOPQRSTUVWXYZ

In the last line, two variants are combined to make an **ultra-bold italic** font. Ultra- or extra- means that the variant has been carried to an extreme.

In recent years, the term font has become confused. In phototypesetting and digital systems, it is often used for a single set of matrixes from which different sizes of type can be produced. Digital systems can also slant, extend and condense characters to almost any degree from a single matrix.

In addition to the font characters, there is a vast collection of characters that do not belong to specific typefaces. They are called **special characters**, **special sorts**, or **pi fonts**, and may include:

Technical symbols, such as algebraic and statistical signs, scientific symbols, liturgical symbols, meteorological symbols, and even the signs of the Zodiac.

Printer's signs, such as raised and centered dots, bullets, quads, boxes, and the familiar pointing finger, known as a **printer's fist**.

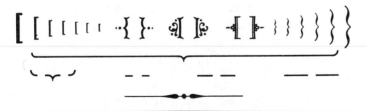

Rules, **brackets**, and **braces**, plain and fancy. Rules are specified in points or fractions of points; 1/4 point rules are sometimes called **hairlines**, and 1/2 point rules, **fine rules**. Rules that thicken toward the middle are called **swelled rules**, and dashed rules are **coupon rules**.

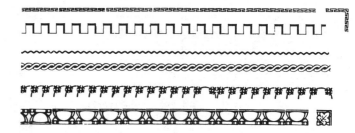

Ornamental **borders** and **corner pieces** for making decorative frames.

Printer's flowers or **fleurons**, which are single, free-standing ornaments that can be used alone or combined into rules, borders or other decorative elements.

Decorative sorts and symbols are often referred to collectively as **dingbats**.

Most typesetters do not keep large collections of special sorts, although, with the advent of digital typesetting, they are becoming more widely available. Usually, a typesetter will keep one 'generic' font for serif types and one for sans serif types. The larger firms, on the other hand, may have a very varied inventory, including such obscure items as circled and canceled numbers, chess characters and the like.

абгдезхуиклмнјопгрњстѕьцӏв

אבגדהוזחטיכדלמםנןסעפףצךקרשׂשׁת

कखगघङङचछजझञटठडढणतथदधन

And then there are the nonroman alphabets . . .

As you might have guessed, there is a specialized vocabulary connected with the design of the type alphabet.

The printed components of the characters that surround the counters are **stems** or **strokes**. The major strokes are **main stems**, or **thick strokes** if there are variations in the thickness of the stems. The other strokes—logically, for once—are **thin strokes**, or **hairlines** if they are very thin. The thinnest part of a curve is also a hairline.

Horizontal or slanted strokes are **arms**, unless they point down, in which case they are **tails**. The Q also has a tail. Short horizontal strokes joining main stems are **crossbars**.

The rounded elements of lower-case characters are **bowls**, except for the lower part of the g, which is a **loop**, joined to the upper bowl by a **link**. The bowl is decorated with an **ear**, as is the stem of the r. It may seem excessive to use four terms to describe a single character, but lower-case g's are perhaps the

A bouquet of serifs, showing only a tiny sample of the forms that serifs take.

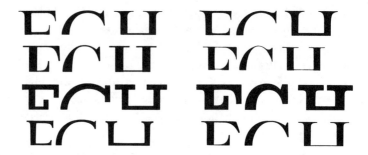

most variegated characters in the type alphabet. When you are trying to identify an unfamiliar face, compare its lower-case g with the specimens in your type books and usually you will be able to pinpoint it in minutes.

The free-standing ends of characters are **terminals**, or **finials** if they are hooked. The points where slanted strokes meet are **apexes**, even when they point down.

In many typefaces, the terminals end in crosspieces called **serifs**. Serifs range from simple, straight hairlines to wedges to slabs and may be merged into the stems with **brackets**.

The characters stand on an imaginary line called the **base-line**. The upper-case charactes are all virtually the same size and reach up to the **cap line**. In contrast, the lower-case characters vary considerably in size and shape.

Fourteen lower-case characters are single-component letters, roughly the same height as the "x". They align at the top on the **mean line** or **x-line**. Actually, only the "x" runs exactly from the baseline to the mean line; the other thirteen have

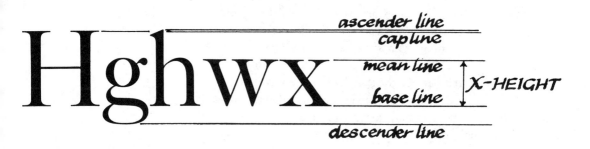

curved or pointed elements that overlap the lines slightly so that they appear to be the same size as the "x". Similarly, vertical strokes look thinner than horizontal strokes of exactly the same thickness. Type designers have learned to thin down the horizontals so they are optically consistent with the upright strokes. You will notice the difference only if you turn the characters on their backs, like this:

EHT ɯⵏⵏ

Seven lower-case characters—b, d, f, h, k, l, and t—have **ascenders** reaching up above the x-line to, or slightly above, the cap line. The last five—g, j, p, q, and y—have **descenders** dropping below the baseline.

The distance between the baseline and the x-line is called the **x-height** of the type, and it may be the most important characteristic of the face since—in general—the taller the x-height, the more readable the face.

There are three other terms describing type faces that are more difficult to define; **weight**, **shading**, and **color**. In fact, many people use them interchangeably, but they describe aspects of type that are of major interest to the designer.

Weight refers to the relative thickness of the elements of a typeface as compared to other typefaces of the same point size. It is probably easier to see the difference than to describe it, so here are a lightweight, medium-weight and heavyweight face:

Shading refers to the way the weight is distributed over the letter-forms. Some typefaces have very thick main stems with hairline thins; some have only minor differences in the thickness

43

of the strokes; others have no apparent difference. Here are four contrasting examples:

Shaded faces are sometimes referred to as **two-weights**; unshaded faces are called **monoweights**.

Weight and shading combine to give type its color. Color re-

Garamond
After experiments with several of the type faces made by the machine companies it was felt that none of them was as suitable as the reproduction of a type cut by a Hollander, Anton Janson, between 1660 and 1687—less than a hundred years after Shakespeare's time.

Baskerville
After experiments with several of the type faces made by the machine companies it was felt that none of them was as suitable as the reproduction of a type cut by a Hollander, Anton Janson, between 1660 and 1687—less than a hundred years after Shakespeare's time.

Goudy O.S.
After experiments with several of the type faces made by the machine companies it was felt that none of them was as suitable as the reproduction of a type cut by a Hollander, Anton Janson, between 1660 and 1687—less than a hundred years after Shakespeare's time.

Bodoni
After experiments with several of the type faces made by the machine companies it was felt that none of them was as suitable as the reproduction of a type cut by a Hollander, Anton Janson, between 1660 and 1687—less than a hundred years after Shakespeare's time.

fers to the general impression of the type block. Lighter faces tend to look grey en masse; heavier, monoweight faces look black. Some contrasting examples are shown below (and the difference will be more obvious if you squint at them):

Weight and shading are inherent in the design of the face. As a designer, you can't do much about them although you can exploit them to create the effect you want on the reader. On the other hand, you can control color to some extent; for example, by adding plenty of line space or setting the type on shorter measures.

Rockwell
After experiments with several of the type faces made by the machine companies it was felt that none of them was as suitable as the reproduction of a type cut by a Hollander, Anton Janson, between 1660 and 1687—less than a hundred years after Shakespeare's time.

Melior
After experiments with several of the type faces made by the machine companies it was felt that none of them was as suitable as the reproduction of a type cut by a Hollander, Anton Janson, between 1660 and 1687—less than a hundred years after Shakespeare's time.

Optima
After experiments with several of the type faces made by the machine companies it was felt that none of them was as suitable as the reproduction of a type cut by a Hollander, Anton Janson, between 1660 and 1687—less than a hundred years after Shakespeare's time.

Univers
After experiments with several of the type faces made by the machine companies it was felt that none of them was as suitable as the reproduction of a type cut by a Hollander, Anton Janson, between 1660 and 1687—less than a hundred years after Shakespeare's time.

45

Type color can be modified by linespacing. The solid Univers at top is a fairly black type, but becomes medium-gray when 3 points of linespacing are added.

The amount of leading that a page requires depends on so many factors that it is difficult to give any fixed method of procedure. The kind of type, the size of type, the length of line and the general character of the text all bear on this point.

The amount of leading that a page requires depends on so many factors that it is difficult to give any fixed method of procedure. The kind of type, the size of type, the length of line and the general character of the text all bear on this point.

Although the terms are a little vague, they define characteristics of type that have an immediate effect on the reader, so you need to be aware of them.

STAGE DIRECTIONS Everyone complains about paperwork, and designers are no exception. Record-keeping apart, you will go through an unbelievable amount of paper before you finish any job. Most of it will be used up in **layouts**.

Layout in the singular is the term used to describe the way you arrange type and graphics in the allotted space. A layout, on the other hand, is the physical blueprint you prepare in planning the layout. As your planning progresses, you will probably produce a series of layouts, each more precise than the one before.

Most designers start with rough sketches called **thumbnails**. Thumbnails are trial sketches, or first attempts at giving shape to the design concept. They are drawn smaller than the finished piece, but always in proportion. Some of the thumbnails for the cover of this book are shown on the next page.

As you can see, some of them look nothing like the actual cover; I was simply trying out various approaches.

When you have found a satisfactory plan, you scale up your thumbnail to a **rough layout**, drawn to actual size in pencil, crayon or felt-tip marker.

Finally, you refine the rough layout into a **finished layout, or finish,** with every element drawn in carefully as it will ap-

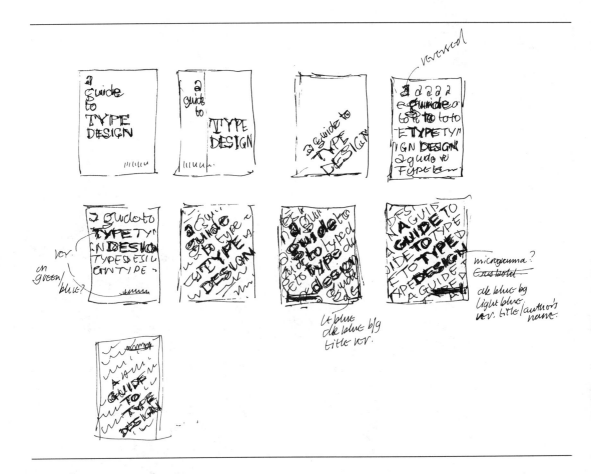

pear, and where it will appear, in the printed version. With any kind of display, you should always send the typesetter or the printer a finished layout.

If you need a client's approval, you may carry the finish one stage further to a **comprehensive** layout or **comp**. In the comp, the main type elements are drawn very precisely in ink or laid down with press type. Blocks of text are shown as greeked type which is garbled type that looks like the real thing. Graphics should also be fairly polished drawings, often converted into photostats. And, if you plan to use color, you also show the actual colors in the comp. In effect, it should be as close to the finished product as you can make it.

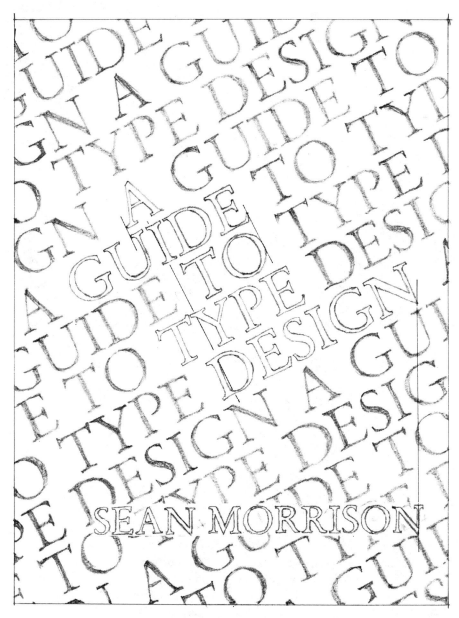

Title type 68/72 Garamond caps, author 30pt Garamond caps Main title & author reversed; remaining type PMS 284; background PMS 287

The finished layout for the cover of this book and, opposite, the mechanical. The reversed type for the author's name and shelfback were added on an overlay and aligned with a set of registration marks matching the three on this mechanical.

Generally, comps are prepared for single-sheet designs, such as advertisements, book covers and posters. If you are working on a booklet or a package design, you may produce a **dummy** instead. A dummy is really a three-dimensional comp that looks like the printed product in every detail.

None of these layouts includes the actual type. By the time you have reached the rough layout stage, however, you have probably decided on the type you want to use and have sent the manuscript or copy to the typesetter with your type specifications.

You will get back a set of proofs, usually known as **galley proofs**. (Galleys were long metal trays in which the type was stored until it was divided into pages and sent to the press.)

In galleys, the type is set in long consecutive segments, normally without any indication of page-breaks. If you are working with a long text, you may set the heads in position, or **in galleys**, as it is called. Often, however, displays are set separately from the text, **as patches**, if they are to be cut apart and pasted into a mechanical.

After you proofread and correct the galleys, you return them to the typesetter. With text galleys, you will also show where you want the page-breaks or column-breaks by drawing a line through the type at the appropriate points. If there are a lot of errors, you may ask for **revised** or **corrected galleys**.

With a longer text, the next step will be **page proofs**, which will include **running heads** (the descriptive heads like those at the top of this page), captions, footnotes and folios. These also have to be proofread carefully, particularly the beginnings and ends of pages to make sure that no text has been dropped by the typesetter.

The final stage, if you are making a mechanical, is the **reproduction proof**, or **repro**, printed on high quality paper. The mechanical is the final artwork that will be used by the printer to make the printing plate. The repros are cut apart and pasted exactly in position along with your line art. (Line art is artwork without any gradations of tone, such as an ink drawing or an engraving. Continuous tone art, such as photographs or paintings, has to be processed separately into halftones by the printer. It is never pasted into the mechanical.)

The printer will also send you a set of proofs to show you that the type and artwork are all where they are supposed to be. These proofs go under a bewildering variety of names— blues, browns, brunings, vandykes, bromides, silvers and others. (Each variety also has its own individual, and often obnoxious, smell depending on the process used to produce it.) They are all cheap, single-color prints intended to give you a final check on your product. Don't be disturbed by the color of the proof; your final version will be printed in the colors you specified.

The blues (or whatever) may arrive in the form of a dummy, which makes life simpler for you. They may also arrive in

A typical imposition for a 16-page signature and the folded sheet. The upper rows of pages would be printed bottom-up from this viewpoint.

sheets, showing how the pages are **imposed**, or arranged for printing. In that case, the order of the pages will be higgledy-piggledy. Don't expect to find Page 1 on the same sheet as Page 2; when it is printed, it will be on the opposite side of the sheet from Page 2. In fact, if you find Page 1 next to Page 2, you had better call the printer immediately. Something has gone really wrong.

Pages are usually imposed in groups of sixteen, or thirty-two for longer text. The minimum imposition is four pages; you can't have a thirty-one page booklet, or a ten-page booklet for that matter. (Actually, you can have a ten-pager, but you will pay the price for the extra work and wasted paper.) The sheet is folded mechanically after it is printed into a **signature**, and the outer edges of the pages are trimmed to the exact size (from which we get the term "trim size" for the actual size of the page).

If you have color illustrations, you will be sent another set of proofs, called **progressive proofs**, which show you each of the four process colors printed separately and in all the combinations up to the final four-color version.

It takes years of experience to "read" four-color proofs and specify corrections to the printer. I have learned to return them with very precise instructions, on the order of "I don't think the dog should be green; please fix." If you haven't had the technical training, I suggest you follow my example: make an appointment with the printer and discuss the problems face to face.

3 CHOOSING A TYPEFACE

Mergenthaler's current catalog lists almost 400 typefaces—if we exclude the non-roman alphabets—in more than 1,700 variants. The Compugraphic Corporation's catalog has almost 300 faces with about 1,000 variants, and very few duplications of the Mergenthaler collection. And these are just two of the major inventories of typefaces available today. I doubt if anybody knows exactly how many there are, but each of them has a unique personality and impact on the reader, so the choice of the right typeface is critical to the design.

Choosing a typeface has never been easy, even for an experienced designer. Many years ago, when the choices were more limited than they are now, W. A. Dwiggins, one of the giants of American typography, wrote "What type shall I use? The gods refuse to answer. They refuse because they do not know."

Innumerable attempts have been made to solve the problem by arranging typefaces into some sort of logical taxonomy, but none has been really successful. The difficulty is that the evolution of the type alphabet has not been a neat, orderly progression. Older faces are often recut and reissued in slightly different forms, and designers constantly hark back to earlier models for inspiration. Dwiggins' most popular face, Caledonia, appeared in 1938, but it was consciously patterned on the Scotch Roman faces of the early eighteenth century. Similarly, the great workhorse Caslon, which was originally designed in the 1720s, has gone through a dozen or more reincarnations in the last hundred years. American Typefounders produced its anomalous Caslon Antique in 1897; Mergenthaler cut Caslon No. 3 in

1913 and Caslon Old Face in 1921 for its Linotype machines; the Haas foundry added its own Caslon to the collection in 1944; and then there are Caslon 76, Caslon No. 223, Caslon 540 and probably several others that I have forgotten about. Do the later versions belong in the same category as the originals? You could probably argue the point from now until Doomsday without finding a satisfactory answer.

Happily, from the working designer's point of view, the hair-splitting can be left to the purists. Many designers get by with a much simpler approach.

The fact is that most typefaces are similar to many other faces, and similar typefaces will produce pretty much the same effect on the reader. There is rarely one—and only one—perfect typeface for any job. If you handed the same project to any six designers, they would probably pick half a dozen different, but perfectly appropriate, faces for the job.

In any case, there are often purely practical restrictions on your choice. The "ideal" face may not be available on the typesetting system you are using, or it may prove to be too wide-setting for the space available. If you can't use your first choice, you can almost always find something very similar in the same family of faces.*

Family resemblances are the result of three forces that always prescribe the designer's creativity in any period—taste, task, and technology.

As we have seen, type people are conservative, professionally if not personally. They tend to follow, rather than to lead, the esthetic bandwagon. And with reason. Good design is unobtrusive design. A design that attracts attention inevitably distracts the reader, and nothing attracts attention like the unaccustomed and the innovative. Consequently, designers work, as a rule, within the bounds of esthetic propriety for their period and are reluctant to accept innovations until everybody else has accepted

---

* The term "family" is sometimes used to define all the different fonts or different cuts of a single design. The various fonts of Helvetica shown in Chapter 2 would constitute part of the Helvetica family; some people would also describe the different cuts of Caslon on Page 56 as members of the Caslon family. I am using the term here in a much broader sense to define all of the typefaces designed on much the same general principles.

them. Gutenberg may have perfected a technology that changed western culture, but his proudest boast was that nobody could tell the difference between his books and the familiar handwritten manuscripts of his time.

Type is also functional in another sense. Print has always been a commercial enterprise; books were the first mass-produced consumer commodity. Typographers, then, are rarely influenced by the art-for-art's-sake syndrome that often afflicts other artists. Nobody designs a typeface just to satisfy a creative itch. New typefaces are designed to compete with other faces already on the market or to meet a new demand in the market. As new tasks have developed for print, new type families have evolved to meet them.

Finally, the designer's work remains an abstraction until it is converted into the printed image, a process that involves a number of technologies—type manufacturing, typesetting, printing and papermaking. The designer of a typeface must be familiar with all of them and work within their limitations. There is little point in producing a typeface that nobody can print. For example, until well into the eighteenth century, paper was made by hand and was a fairly rough-surfaced material by our standards. It had to be soaked to accept a printed image, and the type socked, or punched slightly, into the surface. Consequently, the early designers avoided hairlines, which would not register consistently, and heavy thick stems, which would be likely to blur when they were punched into the sheet.

Perhaps because of these restrictions, typefaces, more than any other artifact, capture the style of their period and reflect it back to later generations of readers, even when those readers know little or nothing about the era in which the designs were created.

In this chapter, I have tried to define briefly the taste, tasks and technologies that have shaped six major familes of typefaces:

Oldstyles, which are the faces produced from about 1500 to the middle of the eighteenth century, whose letter-forms were influenced by quill-written script forms

Transitionals, a small family representing the changeover from script-based letter-forms to purely typographic alphabets

Moderns, the first purely typographic faces

Square serifs, the nineteenth-century faces designed both for display and for text

Sans serifs, the functional typefaces of the twentieth century

Decoratives, a heterogeneous collection of faces designed essentially to be eye-catching rather than readable.

In describing these families, I have made no attempt to discriminate between original faces of the period and later faces patterned on them. It can be argued that Dwiggins was a twentieth-century designer, influenced by the taste, tasks, and technology of his time, but it seems to me that Caledonia was a deliberate throwback, intended to recreate the mood and style of its model. It is certainly closer in flavor to Scotch Roman than to the square serif Stymie or the sans serif Futura which were also designed in the 1930s.

I have also had to ignore the many variations of standard faces produced by different manufacturers, some of which do not seem to have much in common beyond the name. Here, for instance, are three "Caslons".

abcdefghijklmnopqrstuvwxyz
ABCDEFGHIJKLMNOPQRSTUVWXYZ

abcdefghijklmnopqrstuvwxyz
ABCDEFGHIJKLMNOPQRSTUVWXYZ

abcdefghijklmnopqrstuvwxyz
ABCDEFGHIJKLMNOPQRSTUVWXYZ

There simply is not enough room to include them all. As far as possible, I have shown the version I am most familiar with or that, in my opinion, most closely resembles the original. (Another point to keep in mind is that few originals have survived and most of the typefaces we use now are relatively recent recuttings.)

Many contemporary designs appear under a bewildering variety of pseudonyms, in part, it is sad to say, because manufacturers pirate designers' work and issue the face with minor modifications under their own proprietary name. I have, in every case, identified the faces by their original names and included the alternative names in my comments; I can't promise however that the lists are exhaustive. The index will help you to find the original if you know only the pseudonym.

This chapter is intended to be an introduction to the rich collection of typefaces available to the contemporary designer with some comments on the characteristics of the faces. Eventually, as a designer, you will collect your own library of specimen books, which will be far more useful, and develop your own particular taste in type.

In the meantime, I should warn you that this is an eclectic sampling in two respects. First, the bulk of the samples are faces with which I can claim a working relationship. It is as impossible to talk intelligently about a face you haven't used as it is to write a review of a play you haven't seen. (I have followed the same general principle in the bibliography.) However, I have included a handful of faces that are widely popular but that I doubt I would use myself. You will almost certainly be able to tell the difference from my comments. But this is by no means an exhaustive type encyclopedia and may not even be representative.

Second, the 'character studies' of the families and faces represent my own judgements exclusively. You may—and probably will—disagree with some or all of them, but there is plenty of leeway for disagreement in type design. That is one of its endless attractions. And I offer the comments with no more apology than that.

In describing the development of the families, I have attempted briefly to place each in its context of taste, task and technology. However, I have focussed on two critical structural features of the design: the proportions of the characters, and the shading. I was introduced to this approach by David Gates of Pratt Institute and have found it a highly successful way to define the characteristics of the type families. I acknowledge the debt herewith.

THE OLDSTYLES

The oldstyles are a large and very varied family of faces produced from the early sixteenth to the early eighteenth centuries, along with the many faces designed later on the same pattern.

The early oldstyles were modeled closely on the Jenson roman. They are usually referred to as Venetian old styles, because Jenson's press was established in Venice. Italian printers dominated the field for several decades after Jenson, but subsequently Italian typography deteriorated and their place was taken by French typographers. The Venetian faces were handsome, but their French successors were more sharply cut and elegant. For a time, they were widely imitated.

Eventually, however, their popularity also faded, and the lead was taken by Dutch and English designers, who produced sturdy, no-nonsense types, known—not surprisingly—as Dutch/English oldstyles.

A face that typifies the old style in general is Garamond, also known as Garastar, GD, and Grenada, which has been used to set this section of the text.

abcdefghijklmnopqrstuvwxyz

ABCDEFGHIJKLMNOPQRSTUVWXYZ

1234567890(.,:;!?''—/$-%)

abcdefghijklmnopqrstuvwxyz

ABCDEFGHIJKLMNOPQRSTUVWXYZ

1234567890(.,:;!?''—/$-%)

Claude Garamond, who designed the original of this face, was born around 1480. He produced many of his typefaces for the royal press of France. Although he modeled his roman on the types produced by Aldus Manutius, his faces, unlike the earlier Italian faces, owe a great deal less to handwritten forms. He also designed the first face with companion roman and italic fonts, and the first slanted italic caps. Although his designs were widely copied, he died in poverty in 1561, and his punches and types were scattered throughout Europe. Few have survived. Most modern Garamonds, like this one, are based, not on the original design, but on a version cut by a Swiss designer, Jean Jannon, around 1615.

The oldstyle alphabets derive in the long run from the Roman square capitals, whose proportions were retained in the Carolingian miniscule and the Renaissance roman script, which was the immediate model for the oldstyles. The Romans were an orderly, logical people, and applied the same logical approach to the design of their alphabets as they did to all their institutions and inventions. The letterforms are based on right geometrical figures—the square, the circle, and the equilateral triangle. As a result, the capitals particularly vary arbitrarily in width. For example, the M and the N fit into squares of the same size, as do the other 'single-story', straight-sided characters. Similarly, the single-story round characters fit into the circle circumscribed by the square. Two-story characters, such as the E and S, on the other hand, are built on squares or circles stacked one on the other and are consequently only half as wide.

Renaissance designers tried to reconcile this strictly geometric approach with the proportions of the human figure, which was their ideal form. Leonardo da Vinci's well-known "spreadeagled man" whose arms and legs form the radii of a circle and circumscribed square is only one of many attempts to illustrate the relationship. In fact, the search for a purely geometrical method of designing characters kept type designers fairly busy through the first centuries of type. The royal French press, for which Garamond worked, eventually came up with an official set of ideal characters, drawn with T-square and compasses, on a grid of 2,304 squares.

Obviously, no designer is going to work strictly to a set of arbitrary mathematical rules, but all oldstyle designers stuck to letterforms based on circles and squares, so much so that these proportions are generally known as oldstyle proportions.

Most oldstyles have fairly low x-heights and long ascenders and descenders. The caps are usually shorter than the ascenders, particularly in the older faces like Garamond.

The serifs are fairly heavy with full brackets that often run the length of the serif. Finials usually end with completely triangular serifs, as in the Garamond C, S, and T. In the earlier faces, the serifs are often cupped or slightly curved; in fact, a good clue to the age of an old style is the amount of curvature. By the eighteenth century, the serifs are almost dead straight and the brackets are less heavy.

The oldstyles are all two-weight alphabets, although the difference between thicks and thins is not marked. The letters had to print clearly on handmade paper, which was not particularly smooth, so they were punched slightly into the surface. Consequently, the designers avoided heavy thicks, which would have tended to smear, and true hairlines, which would not print clearly and consistently.

The shading of the characters, in fact, is very close to the shading of script letters written with a chisel-edged quill pen. A quill pen ends in a flat point, to distribute the ink, and it is held at a slight angle so that it does not catch in the weave of the paper and splutter ink. As a result, neither the vertical nor the horizontal strokes are the full width of the pen. Curved letters, on the other hand, are the full width at their widest points and taper off smoothly almost to hairlines.

The slant of the quill also produces a backward-leaning shading, or optical axis, which is also typical of oldstyle letters.

uerum eg
verum

The shading of Times Roman matches almost exactly the shading of the quill-formed script above, even though it is a twentieth-century oldstyle.

Oldstyles, then, are slightly irregular, both in the proportions and the shading of the letters. They have much in common with script. They stagger, rather than march, across the page. But this irregularity is not a shortcoming; it gives them warmth and humanity, often allied with grace and elegance. More importantly, from the type designer's viewpoint, it makes them highly readable. Oldstyles form very distinctive and variegated word-shapes, which are the key to fluent reading. The lack of strong contrast in the shading also gives them a restful, medium-gray color when they are set in blocks of running text.

Oldstyles are, above all else, text faces. They were designed primarily as book faces and still serve the purpose admirably.

Their shading and proportions, however, make it difficult to condense, extend, or boldface them. If you change the proportions of a square or circle, it automatically ceases to be a square or circle and the basic proportions of the letters are distorted. The face, in effect, is no longer an oldstyle. Similarly, if you beef up or thin down the thick strokes, the characters lose their distinctively calligraphic appearance. (Even italicizing presents problems with oldstyles, since the forward slant of the characters tends to conflict with the backward slant of the shading. Many oldstyles have unsatisfactory italics.)

Most oldstyles, then, make less than perfect display faces. Few, in fact, were originally supplied with anything but roman and italic fonts, and later attempts to graft bold faces and other variants onto them have rarely been successful. Some modern oldstyles, such as Times Roman, however, have been designed with a full range of compatible fonts.

61

Here are a small sample of other oldstyles, illustrating the wide and varied range in this family.

abcdefghijklmnopqrstuvwxyz
ABCDEFGHIJKLMNOPQRSTUVWXYZ

Bembo is the Venetian granddaddy of the oldstyles. The original was cut by Griffo some years before the Aldine italic. It is a crisp, strong, elegant face, with an almost chiselled look. The x-height is low and the ascenders and descenders long, so that Bembo always has an airy appearance, even though it is a tight-setting face. Several cuts of the face have been supplied with variant fonts, including some of the ugliest boldfaces produced anywhere. We would be better off without them. (Bembo is also known as Aldine Roman, Bem, and Griffo.)

abcdefghijklmnopqrstuvwxyz
ABCDEFGHIJKLMNOPQRSTUVWXYZ

Caslon is one of the last authentic oldstyles. It was designed by William Caslon, who started to produce typefaces about 1725. This face, except for a short period in the nineteenth century, has been immensely popular since it first appeared. Benjamin Franklin was one of its many fans, which may account for the fact that the Declaration of Independence was set in Caslon. Taken letter by letter, it is full of flaws, but it hangs together beautifully. "When in doubt, use Caslon" is one of the oldest cliches in type design. (Also Caslostar)

abcdefghijklmnopqrstuvwxyz
ABCDEFGHIJKLMNOPQRSTUVWXYZ

Cloister is an almost deliberately old-fashioned looking Venetian, designed by Morris Benton at the end of the last century. It has the characteristic low x-height and heavily slanted shading, but is more evenly weighted than the original Venetians. (Also Eusebius, Ludlow)

abcdefghijklmnopqrstuvwxyz
ABCDEFGHIJKLMNOPQRSTUVWXYZ

Electra is a typically honest, unobtrusive face by W. A. Dwiggins, with no eccentricities. One of the most readable of text faces, the original had both an attractive italic and a slanted roman. It is a light face. Dwiggins' designs are akin to Colonial architecture; they are so serviceable and unassuming that it is easy to overlook their perfect balance. When in doubt, use Dwiggins. (Also Elante, Selectra)

abcdefghijklmnopqrstuvwxyz
ABCDEFGHIJKLMNOPQRSTUVWXYZ

Goudy Old Style was designed by the doyen of American designers, Frederic W. Goudy, in 1915. It is a Venetian, but with a larger x-height than most and unusually short descenders, which Goudy subsequently considered a flaw. Apparently many contemporary designers would not agree since the face is still popular. The deficiency, in any case, is counterbalanced by the handsome upper case, based on a Renaissance square capital, which makes a good display face in its own right.

abcdefghijklmnopqrstuvwxyz
ABCDEFGHIJKLMNOPQRSTUVWXYZ

Granjon was designed by an English printer, George W. Jones, and issued by Mergenthaler in 1928. Although named for a contemporary of Garamond, it is in fact a virtual reproduction of a genuine Garamond roman that appeared in 1592. The caps are larger than Bembo's, but it is a lighter face than either Bembo or the so-called Garamonds. It also has the typical elegance and snap of the French oldstyles, but appreciates generous linespacing.

abcdefghijklmnopqrstuvwxyz
ABCDEFGHIJKLMNOPQRSTUVWXYZ

Janson is misnamed for an influential Dutch typefounder, Anton Janson; it was in fact designed by the Hungarian Miklos Kís about 1690. Nevertheless, it is the epitome of the Dutch style: sturdy, plain, and straightforward. The x-height is comparatively large, and the shading heavier and more contrasty than in most old styles, giving Janson an unusual snap and sparkle. It has long been a workhorse in book design.

abcdefghijklmnopqrstuvwxyz
ABCDEFGHIJKLMNOPQRSTUVWXYZ

Palatino is a broad, dark calligraphic face in the French style. It was designed in 1950 by Herman Zapf, perhaps the greatest of contemporary type designers. It is a more even, uniform design than most oldstyles, and one of the few that can stand up to display sizes. As a text face, it is perhaps a bit bland. (Also Andover, Elegante, Malibu, Palastar, Palladium, Patina, Pontiac. Emulation is the sincerest form of flattery.)

abcdefghijklmnopqrstuvwxyz
ABCDEFGHIJKLMNOPQRSTUVWXYZ

Perpetua, the text face for this book, is a broad, open, sharply cut Venetian by the English designer Eric Gill (who was, among many other things, a stone-cutter). It strongly resembles Bembo; in fact, you can think of it as a wider-setting version of its model. (Also Percepta, Perpetual)

abcdefghijklmnopqrstuvwxyz
ABCDEFGHIJKLMNOPQRSTUVWXYZ

Times Roman was designed under the direction of Stanley Morison for *The Times* of London. It is a bold, black Dutch/English face but its generous x-height and plain letter-forms

64

make it eminently readable. Inexplicably, *The Times* dropped it in 1975, but it remains a standard elsewhere. It has, unusually, an excellent boldface. (Also English, English Times, London Roman, Pegasus, Press Roman, Times New Roman, Times Star and TR)

abcdefghijklmnopqrstuvwxyz
ABCDEFGHIJKLMNOPQRSTUVWXYZ

Weiss is a slightly eccentric face, designed by Emir Rudolf Weiss in 1926. The uneven shading and abrupt serifs give it a consciously antique look, and it always seems to have been assembled by a not-very-skilled typesetter. Despite its oddities, however, it is a very readable face. (Also Edelweiss)

THE TRANSITIONALS

The transitionals are a small group of faces, forming a bridge between the essentially calligraphic oldstyles and the purely typographic modern faces that began to appear in the late eighteenth century. This is Baskerville, a typical transitional, and the face in which this section has been set. (It is also known as Baskerline, Baskerstar, Beaumont and BR.)

abcdefghijk lmnopqrstuvwxyz
ABCDEFGHIJKLMNOPQRSTUVWXYZ
1234567890(.,:;!?''—/$-%)

abcdefghijklmnopqrstuvwxyz
ABCDEFGHIJKLMNOPQRSTUVWXYZ
1234567890(.,:;!?''—/$-%)

The English typefounder John Baskerville issued the original of this face in 1780. Baskerville started his career as a writing master—an expert in the new script called copperplate. Copperplate, as its name implies, was an engraver's script, produced with a needle-pointed burin on a metal plate, but it quickly became popular as a general script. Copperplate was written with a sharp offset pen, which produced fine hairlines; shading was created by increasing and decreasing pressure on the point. Its curves are artificially mathematical, and the thicker swells of the strokes are more abrupt and less tapered than those formed by a flat-cndcd quill. Obviously, Baskerville had a taste for hairlines, and was largely responsible for producing a paper that would carry them. Among his other innovations, he was the first to calendar, or smooth, paper by pressing it between heated copper plates.

He turned from calligraphy to the japanning trade, made himself a fortune, and then lost it after he moved into typefounding at the age of 40 because his types could not compete with Caslon's, at least in England. The difference between Baskerville and Caslon does not seem striking to us, but at the time people found the new face too dry and heavy. In fact, transitionals share many of the features of oldstyles, but the small differences were to pave the way for a major revolution in the type alphabet.

Transitionals are designed to oldstyle, uneven-width proportions. Their serifs, however, are thinner, sharper and flatter. Frequently, they taper off into hairlines.

The shading of the transitionals is quite different. Thick strokes are heavier, thin strokes are generally lighter, and the shading is less noticeably slanted to the left. As a result, transitionals are generally heavier and more upright than their predecessors, with a sharper contrast in their weighting.

Cumulatively, the difference is striking. Transitionals have more authority than oldstyles and produce a more uniform page, without the charmingly uneven appearance of the oldstyles. They generally prefer more white space around them. Baskerville used plenty of leading and generous margins, which were also unpopular innovations in his day.

Here are several more transitionals.

abcdefghijklmnopqrstuvwxyz
ABCDEFGHIJKLMNOPQRSTUVWXYZ

Bulmer was designed about 1790 by Baskerville's pupil William Martin for William Bulmer's Shakespeare Press. It is a leaner, lighter face than Baskerville, with more irregular weighting that gives it a sort of country-town job printer's look.

abcdefghijklmnopqrstuvwxyz
ABCDEFGHIJKLMNOPQRSTUVWXYZ

Fairfield, designed by Rudolf Ruzicka and issued in 1939, is something of a hybrid. It has the weight and regularity of a transitional, but it also has markedly old-style features—notably the long ascenders and descenders. Its blending of humanistic warmth and transitional uniformity made it a popular text face in the decades after World War II, but it is rarely used today. It should be about due for a revival.

abcdefghijklmnopqrstuvwxyz
ABCDEFGHIJKLMNOPQRSTUVWXYZ

Fournier is perhaps the first transitional, designed by the Fournier who gave us the point. It is much lighter than other transitionals, and narrower than most, with smoother, less-angular curves.

abcdefghijklmnopqrstuvwxyz
ABCDEFGHIJKLMNOPQRSTUVWXYZ

Nobody knows who designed Scotch Roman, but it is clearly based on faces cut by Richard Austin about 1810. It is difficult to decide, in fact, whether this should be called the last of the transitionals or an early modern. It has the cool balance of the latter, but still retains the warmth of the former. The classification really doesn't matter; it remains a straightforward, highly readable face with a touch of elegance.

THE MODERNS "Moderns" may seem a odd term for typefaces that first appeared in the eighteenth century, but the decades between Caslon and Bodoni saw the emergence of modern western society. Newton and his fellow scientists had forged the empirical principles underlying modern science, and philosophers and political and social theorists, such as Hume, Locke and Adam Smith, had adopted equally pragmatic viewpoints. A rational, mechanical, slightly colder view of the universe and its inhabitants began to take shape. Before the end of the century, the American Revolution ushered in the first democracy, the French Revolution ushered out the last absolute monarchy, and the Industrial Revolution began to displace individual craftwork with mass production, and human muscle with mechanical power.

The arts mirrored this changing world. The ornamental baroque and rococo styles, so closely associated with a leisured aristocracy, were displaced by a strict emphasis on structure and form, inspired by the severe, uncluttered styles of classical Greece and Rome.

In 1789, the year that marked the start of the French Revolution, Mozart completed his forty-first and final symphony, the ultimate classical work; Thomas Jefferson started planning his beloved Monticello with a portico that looked like a classical Greek temple; and Giambattista Bodoni, the Duke of Parma's private printer, produced this typeface, which is named after him (and also BO, Bodoni-star, and Brunswick), and is the typeface for this section.

68

abcdefghijklmnopqrstuvwxyz

ABCDEFGHIJKLMNOPQRSTUVWXYZ

1234567890(.,:;!?"—/$-%)

abcdefghijklmnopqrstuvwxyz

ABCDEFGHIJKLMNOPQRSTUVWXYZ

1234567890(.,:;!?"—/$-%)

Bodoni's was not the first modern typeface; Firmin Didot, the youngest of the family had published the first true modern in 1784. However, Bodoni epitomizes this new family.

The modern alphabet is based rationally on equal-width ellipses and rectangles, not circles and squares. As a result, the capitals are uniform in width, and generally narrower than their oldstyle and transitional counterparts.

The caps are also the same height as the ascenders, and the serifs are reduced to uncompromisingly straight hairlines, usually without brackets in modern recuttings like this.

The weighting of the moderns is correspondingly uniform and balanced. Thin strokes, like the serifs, are simply hairlines, while the thick strokes are fairly heavy and symmetrical. The curved strokes are optically the same width at their widest points as the straight stems, and they narrow abruptly into the hairlines, in sharp contrast to the smoothly tapered curves of the earlier families. The swells, in fact, resemble the artificial swells of copperplate script, shaped by an engraver's tool, not by a pen.

The optical stress has also moved completely to the vertical. There is no hint of a slope in the moderns. The last vestiges of handwritten forms have disappeared. The moderns are the first purely typographic faces.

They are precise, rational, crisply defined—as cool as a Mozart wind quintet and as elegant as a classical Greek frieze. The strong contrasts in weight give them sparkle and brilliance, but they can also be severe and cold. An early critic of the new style complained of their "extreme dryness and absolutely glacial rigidity of line". Both Bodoni and Didot were extremely generous with margins and linespacing in their designs, and presumably they knew their business better than anyone else.

The modern proportions, however, along with the precisely balanced weighting, allow for variation on the basic regular roman. They can be boldfaced or lightened without losing their essential character; they may also be extended and condensed successfully because the horizontal stretching or compressing of an ellipse or a rectangle does not violate its integrity.

Moderns, then, are the first all-purpose faces, equally at home as text or display types. They were designed in a period when mass-production was in its infancy, and advertising, the foster-child of excess consumer goods, was making its modest start. In fact, the moderns, in ultrabold versions called fat faces, supplied the first advertising types. Here is a fat-face version of Bodoni, called Bodoni Poster.

abcdefghijklmnopqrstuvwxyz
ABCDEFGHIJKLMNOPQRSTUVW

Notice that, despite the extreme exaggeration of the

weight, this is still recognizably a scion of the Bodoni stock.

Here are some more moderns.

abcdefghijklmnopqrstuvwxyz
ABCDEFGHIJKLMNOPQRSTUVWXYZ

Caledonia is another deceptively simple Dwiggins design, produced in 1938. The shading is not as contrasty as the original moderns', and the slightly cupped serifs, with their noticeable brackets are not strictly to rule. However, in every essential, this is a modern face, perhaps less severe than most. It is one of the most readable and popular text faces. (Also Caledo, Calendonstar, California, Cornelia, Edinburgh, Gemini, Highland, and Laurel)

abcdefghijklmnopqrstuvwxyz
ABCDEFGHIJKLMNOPQRSTUVWXYZ

Century Expanded is one of the many and varied offspring of an oldstyle face designed by Loyd Benton and Theodore DeVinne for *Century* magazine. Despite its parentage, Century Expanded, which was issued by American Typefounders in 1900, is clearly a modern. It is a dark, unassuming face with a very large x-height, and, despite its name, a fairly tight set. It lacks the elegance of many moderns, but has a great deal of warmth. (Also Cambridge Expanded, CE, Censtar Expanded, Century, Century Light, and Century X)

abcdefghijklmnopqrstuvw
xyzABCDEFGHIJKLMNOP
QRSTUVWXYZ

Craw Modern was designed by Freeman Craw and issued

by American Typefounders in 1958. It is remarkable for its wide set, one of the widest among standard faces, and its very short ascenders and descenders. Despite its mild eccentricities, it is an eminently readable, if dark, face in both the roman and the excellent bold fonts.

abcdefghijklmnopqrstuvwxyz
ABCDEFGHIJKLMNOPQRSTUVWXYZ

The original of DeVinne was cut in 1894 by Gustave Schroeder for the forerunners of American Typefounders, and has spawned a number of recuttings. It is a light, lean face, very similar in many respects to Didot.

abcdefghijklmnopqrstuvwxyz
ABCDEFGHIJKLMNOPQRSTUVWXYZ

Didot is a twentieth-century version of the first modern, designed by Firmin Didot in 1784. It set the pattern for the French moderns that followed. Unlike Bodoni, it is a fairly narrow face, with a smaller x-height and less rigidly uniform weighting. The curved strokes are distinctly bottom heavy and slightly irregular. It is a more human face than Bodoni, but still needs generous linespacing. (Also Didi)

abcdefghijklmnopqrstuvwxyz
ABCDEFGHIJKLMNOPQRSTUVWXYZ

Torino is a contemporary modern in the style of the English moderns. It is a light, sharply cut face with an unusually close set. The abrupt transitions in the shading, exaggerated by the condensed letter-forms, make it dazzling, perhaps too much so for running text.

abcdefghijklmnopqrstuvwxyz
ABCDEFGHIJKLMNOPQRSTUVWXYZ

Walbaum was designed by the German typefounder,

72

Justin Walbaum, early in the nineteenth century. It follows the Didot, rather than the Bodoni, style, but is broader than both. The squarish, slightly squat lower case produces a very even, almost regimented page.

abcdefghijklmnopqrstuvwxyz
ABCDEFGHIJKLMNOPQRSTUVWX

Cooper Black is a twentieth-century fat face, designed expressly as such by Oswald Cooper in the 1920s. It is a big, blobby, cheerful type, with a great deal of warmth and yet a certain amount of authority. Obviously, it is not, and is not intended to be, a text face. (Also Pabst, Pittsburgh Black)

THE SQUARE SERIFS

By the beginning of the nineteenth century, the Industrial Revolution was under way, and the Industrial Revolution begat mass-produced consumer goods, and mass-production begat advertising, and advertising begat the square serifs.

The earlier families were fundamentally text faces, meant to be read at a distance of eighteen inches or so, not at long range. But that was precisely what the new-born advertising and packaging industries wanted as the nineteenth century gathered steam—in every sense of the term.

The first attempts at display faces were the ultrabold fat faces. However, although their thicks were weighted-up dramatically, their modern hairlines remained stubbornly hairline and disappeared at a distance.

The solution was to fatten up the characters overall, and this process led to the development of a new family of types called the square serifs.

The new alphabets may, in fact, have been created by sign-writers and poster painters rather than by type designers. The first typographic square serif was not issued until 1815, although square-serif lettering had begun to appear on store fronts well before that date. In fact, Napoleon's troops had passed along messages from outpost to outpost with oversized square-serif placards, and by 1815 Napoleon was in exile on St. Helena and his armies disbanded.

In a roundabout way, Napoleon was responsible for the

names given to many square serifs. During his Egyptian campaign, his troops discovered the Rosetta Stone, which provided the key to the translation of hieroglyphics and sparked a widespread interest in Egyptian archeology. The early square serifs became known as Egyptians, presumably because their blocky forms reminded people of the heavy, slabby architecture of the Nile Valley. The term is still widely used in Europe.

There are two branches of the family. The first, the two-weight square serifs, are essentially heavy moderns. The second, the monoweight square serifs, with their unvaried weighting, represent a complete departure from the earlier type tradition and point the way to twentieth-century developments.

Two-Weight Square Serifs The typical two-weight square serif is Clarendon, which was issued by the English firm of R. Besley & Co. in 1845. This section is set in Clarendon Book.

abcdefghijklmnopqrstuvwxyz
ABCDEFGHIJKLMNOPQRSTU
VWXYZ
1234567890(.,:;!?"—/$-%)

It is so typical in fact that this whole branch of the square-serif family is sometimes referred to as Clarendons.

Clarendon was originally designed as a special bold face to be used with a modern text type in dictionaries, catalogs and similar publications. Its proportions are the familiar, modern even-width proportions, based on uniform ellipses and rectangles. Like the moderns, the caps are also even with the ascenders. However, the letter-forms are typically much broader than those of the moderns.

The serifs are noticeably longer and stoutly bracketed, but their most distinctive feature is the squared-off ends from which the family takes its name.

Clarendon is also knows as ClarendoStar, Clarion, and Clarique.

The two-weights have the balanced weighting of the moderns, but obviously are much heavier faces. The distinctive hairlines have been replaced by substantial thin strokes and the thick strokes are very heavy.

The two-weight square serifs are a natural extension of the modern design, but they are no longer primarily text faces (although many of them, like Clarendon, are excellent text faces). They are the first of the display faces. Their weight and uniformity, allied to the heavy serifs that form solid foundations on the base line, make them highly visible at any distance. They have presence and authority in any context.

Here are some more of them.

abcdefghijklmnopqrstuvwxyz
ABCDEFGHIJKLMNOPQRSTUVWXYZ

Bookman was designed originally as a boldface for a series of pedestrian Victorian faces called Old Style (which were supposed to substitute for Caslon, then temporarily out of favor). They have, happily, disappeared, while Bookman, happily, survives. It is light for a two-weight, with relatively little contrast in the shading. The ascenders and descenders are short, so that it appears compact, but it has a very generous x-height and set and is highly readable. (Also Bookface)

abcdefghijklmnopqrstuvwxyz
ABCDEFGHIJKLMNOPQRSTUVWXYZ

Century Schoolbook is another offspring of Century, but is nonetheless a square serif. It is not as elegant as many two-weights and fairly tight setting, but it is a sturdy, unobtrusive face. As its name implies, it has frequently been used for children's books because of its high readability. (Also Cambridge Light, Cambridge Schoolbook, Censtar School, Century Medium, Century Modern, Century Text, Century Textbook, CS, and Schoolbook)

abcdefghijklmnopqrstuvwxyz
ABCDEFGHIJKLMNOPQRSTUVWXYZ

Cheltenham was designed by Bertram Goodhue for Linotype in 1896. It quickly became popular, and between the two world wars reigned supreme as the advertising face. It has disproportionately large caps, disproportionately short descenders, eccentrically uneven weighting, stumpy serifs, and a stingy x-height. The reasons for its popularity escape me entirely, but I am obviously in a small minority since its popularity remains undiminished. (Also Cheltonian, Gloucester, Nordhoff, and Winchester).

abcdefghijklmnopqrstuvwxyz
ABCDEFGHIJKLMNQRSTUVWXYZ

Melior is yet another stylish Zapf face, with the characteristic calligraphic style. It is much lighter than most two-weights. It is easily recognized by the unusual rectangular curves that give the face a very even texture. Melior is equally successful as a text and a display face. (Also Ballardvale, Hanover, Lyra, Mallard, ME, Medallion, Melier, Meliostar, Uranus, and Ventura)

abcdefghijklmnopqrstuvwxyz
ABCDEFGHIJKLMNOPQRSTUVWXYZ

Souvenir is another undistinguished design

which is currently immensely popular. It was designed by the prolific Morris Benton (on one of his off days) in 1914. Its design is typical of the slackly curved, art nouveau faces that were widely used in the early years of this century but that have since descended deservedly into oblivion. Souvenir is almost automatically paired with Seagull as a head type. The two are an ideal match for each other.

Monoweight Square Serifs

The next logical step after weighting-up the thins would seem to be weighting them up further until they matched the thicks. That is the usual explanation for the development of the monoweight square serifs. However logic has never been the hallmark of developments in type.

The era in which the monoweight square serifs took shape—the early 1800s—was the era in which mechanical power decisively replaced muscle power. The textile industries led the way with the development of the steam-powered spinning mule, but the first steamship was launched in 1802 and Fulton's *Claremont* went into regular service in 1807. The first steam train rolled eighteen years later. The new power systems demanded frameworks stronger than wood, which had until then been the primary construction material. The nineteenth century was, above all else, the age of iron. Bridges, buildings, machines and vehicles were built of metal and stood or moved on iron underpinnings, all engineered precisely to specification.

The monoweight square serifs have something of the same mechanical structure. The two-weights were a fairly natural progression from the moderns; the monoweights represent a novel approach to the design of the alphabet. They are the first constructed typefaces and represent the initial step toward the functional faces of the twentieth century. It may be significant that none of them is named after its designer; in fact, many of their names have Egyptian associations, perhaps reflecting the growing interest in the new science of archeology.

There were two other significant changes. First, many monoweights have the single-story lower-case a and open-tailed g which had previously been italic forms. And, second, the italic, with its essentially calligraphic forms, is replaced with a slanted roman, another typographic innovation. Stymie, designed by Morris F. Benton in 1931, is a classic monoweight square serif, and has been used to set this section of the text.

abcdefghijklmnopqrstuvwxyz
ABCDEFGHIJKLMNOPQRSTUVWXYZ
1234567890(.,:;!?"—/$-%)

abcdefghijklmnopqrstuvwxyz
ABCDEFGHIJKLMNOPQRSTUVWXYZ
1234567890(.,:;!?"—/$-%)

Stymie's letter-proportions are modern, although—like the two-weight square serifs—the characters are broader than those of the modern faces. There is no apparent variation in the thickness of the strokes; even the squared-off serifs are the same weight as the stems, and they are unbracketed. Unlike most other monoweights, however, Stymie has some minor eccentricities, typical of many of Benton's faces. The G has an exaggerated crossbar, the slanted strokes of the M do not reach the baseline, and the t has a flat foot. The two-story lower-case a is also untypical, but a single-story a is available as an alternative character as the text shows.

More typically, the "italic" is essentially an oblique version of the roman.

Stymie is also known as Alexandria, Cairo, Memphis, Pyramid, Rockwell and ST.

The monoweights are perhaps the most uniform-looking of all typefaces, and very difficult to tell apart. The identification problem has been confounded by an egregious confusion in nomenclature by film and digital type manufacturers. Three of Stymie's pseudonyms, for example—Cairo, Memphis and Rockwell—were originally the names of completely different monoweights.*

The monoweights have a regimented, mechanical appearance particularly in running text, and a very even texture. The unvaried color and the disciplined string of serifs along the baseline sometimes make them uncomfortable text faces. They are primarily display faces, as they were designed to be.

Here are several more.

abcdefghijklmnopqrstuvwxyz
ABCDEFGHIJKLMNOPQRSTUVWXYZ

Beton, which was designed by Heinrich Jost in 1930, is a narrow face with some slight eccentricities (such as the unbalanced serif of the A and the oddly curved C). It is generally closer in feeling to the earlier monoweights than most. The bolder fonts have a massive quality that once proved irresistible to advertising art directors. They have declined in popularity in recent years.

abcdefghijklmnopqrstuvwxyz
ABCDEFGHIJKLMNOPQRSTUVWXYZ

Memphis is the earliest of the modern monoweights. It was designed by Rudolf Wolf in 1929. It is a round, open, light face with short ascenders and descenders and high readability as a text face. (Also Alexandria, Cairo, Pyramid, ST—and, God help us!—Stymie)

---

* Even this version of Stymie is slightly muddled. The Q has been lifted from Memphis! (Take a look at the specimen of Memphis.) The original Stymie Q had a horizontal tail set below the bowl. If this trend continues, presumably we will wind up with just one homogenized monoweight.

abcdefghijklmnopqrstuvwxyz
ABCDEFGHIJKLMNOPQRSTUVWXYZ

Rockwell was issued by the Monotype Corporation in 1934. Many of the most popular monoweights appeared around the same time. It is one of the most uncompromisingly geometric of the monoweights, and heavier in weight than most. The serifs are also fairly long, adding to the regimented look of the face. (Also Memphis, Stymie and presumably any of the other pseudonyms of these and several other monoweights)

abcdefghijklmnopqrstuvwxyz
ABCDEFGHIJKLMNOPQRSTUVWXYZ

Every family has its black sheep. The reverse-weight square serifs, like Branding Iron, are the outcasts of the family. Apparently somebody decided that, if you were going to make the serifs as thick as the stems, you might as well go all the way and make them thicker. It wasn't a particularly good idea. Reverse-weights are inevitably associated with circuses and Wild West shows and they are best left there.

SANS SERIFS If you remove the serifs from a monoweight square serif, you get an alphabet reduced to its simplest, most functional form. In effect you create a sans serif face ("sans" is the French for "without").

The sans serif family may well have originated in just that way. The original was issued in 1816 by William Caslon IV, the last of the Caslons to own the family business. He loathed square serifs and was apparently trying to combat the new trend in type by offering an alternative, but he still called his rather crude creation a "two-line Egyptian".

The experiment was not a success in many respects. A number of sans serifs were produced throughout the nineteenth century, but they were not particularly popular. Worse still,

Caslon's deliberate misnaming of his face (at the time, square serifs were commonly called Egyptians) started a long-lasting confusion in nomenclature. In England, the family was originally called sans surryphs, and then grotesques, the term now generally used in Europe, although there is a growing movement to rename them lineales. In this country, they were first called gothics, and then sans serifs, at which point the term gothics was transferred to the pre-twentieth-century sans serifs. None of the names makes much sense (even sans serifs, since many decorative faces are serifless). However, there isn't any point in adding to the muddle by calling them something else.

The family played second fiddle to other typefaces until just after the first world war, when they found a powerful champion—the Bauhaus. This influential school of design was founded in 1919 by the architect Walter Gropius, who became its first director. Its faculty included such figures as Mies van der Rohe (who succeeded Gropius), Klee and Kandinsky. Their aim was to fuse the creative arts and crafts with modern technology, and, almost automatically, the uncluttered, functional forms of the sans serifs appealed to them. They adopted sans serifs to the exclusion of all other typefaces, and even advocated dispensing with capitals as an unnecessary frill.

San serifs are now one of the predominant type families, and the bulk of new faces to appear in the last thirty years have been sans serifs.

The stripped-down simplicity of the letter-forms is very much in keeping with the age of high technology. The monoweights particularly give the impression that they were designed by a computer. However, the simplicity of these faces gives them great versatility in a period when the tasks of print have proliferated. The letterforms are highly legible in practically any size and can be manipulated almost endlessly without losing their integrity. They can also be frustratingly similar for a new designer. However, the family can be divided into two main branches: the monoweights, whose design was foreshadowed by the monoweight square serifs, and the shaded sans serifs, which represent a return to more humanistic, often calligraphic, letterforms. The monoweights can be further subdivided into two groups on the basis of letter proportions.

The two main branches of the monoweight sans serifs, represented by the uneven-width Futura above and the even-width Univers below.

The first, and smaller, group have oldstyle proportions; the second, and somewhat later, group have modern, even-width proportions.

Uneven-Width Monoweights

The Bauhaus designers and their disciples were not only addicted to functionalism, but also to assymetry. Contradictorally, then, while they advocated stripping letter-forms down to bare-bones simplicity, they also returned to the assymmetrical, uneven-width proportions of the oldstyle designs, as you can see in the model uneven-width monoweight, Futura, in which this section is set.

Futura was designed by Paul Renner in 1927, and is the perfect expression of the Bauhaus idiom. It is simple, direct, absolutely geometric, and almost devoid of distinguishing features, which, in a sense, gives it a unique character. Futura is type taken to the limits of functionalism. It looks as if it has been designed with a slide rule and micrometer gauge.

The oldstyle proportions are most obvious in the curved characters; the lower-case counters are almost perfect circles. However, Futura has several other oldstyle characteristics. The x-height is low, the ascenders and descenders correspondingly long, the caps are shorter than the ascenders, and the cap M is splayed.

The weighting of the letters is almost absolutely uniform.

abcdefghijklmnopqrstuvwxyz
ABCDEFGHIJKLMNOPQRSTUVWXYZ
1234567890(.,:;!?"—/$-%)

abcdefghijklmnopqrstuvwxyz
ABCDEFGHIJKLMNOPQRSTUVWXYZ
1234567890(.,:;!?"—/$-%)

The only obvious shading is the thinning of the lower-case loops where they meet the straight stems.

Futura was so successful that it almost completely discouraged competition. Few designers were willing to challenge its perfect simplicity. Linotype produced a book face called Spartan, but it is so similar to Futura that I have never been able to tell them apart. It is also called Airport, Europe, FU, Futurstar, Photura, Sirius, Techno, Tempo, Twentieth Century, and Utica.

Here are two of its few rivals.

abcdefghijklmnopqrstuvwxyz
ABCDEFGHIJKLMNOPQRSTUVWXYZ

Gill Sans is another sturdy design by Eric Gill. It has been very popular in Europe, but has only recently become widely available here. It is one of the most attractive mono-weights, because there is a hint of shading in the letter-forms, and it is less strictly geometric than Futura. It has several excellent variant forms, including a striking reversed version (Gill Cameo) and a shadowed version. Oddly enough, Gill commented later that it would have looked better with serifs. Not many typographers would agree. (Also Glib, Graphic, Gothic)

83

abcdefghijklmnopqrstuvwxyz
ABCDEFGHIJKLMNOPQRSTUVWXYZ

Rudolf Koch's Kabel, a recutting of a face that appeared when the transatlantic cable was being laid, is probably the closest of the modern sans serifs to the nineteenth-century faces. A narrower face than Futura, it has the typical low x-height and long ascenders, but is otherwise a fairly eccentric design for a monoweight with odd letter-forms, such as the b, angled ends to the main strokes, and diamond-shaped dots on the i and j. (Also Cable, Cabot, and Sans Serif)

Even-Width Monoweights The uneven-width sans serifs are for the purist. They were the first successful members of the family and established sans serifs as a vital part of the type universe. However, their oldstyle proportions limited their versatility to some extent, and they were a little cold-blooded for the post-World War II era. They have gradually been supplanted since the 1950s by the second branch of the monoweights—the even-width monoweights—whose modern proportions give them the full range of flexibility demanded by contemporary design.

One of the most popular even-width monoweights is Adrian Frutiger's aptly named Univers. Like many contemporary designs, it was issued (in 1957) in a complete series of variant fonts, called the Univers palette. Here are two of them; Univers 55, the text face of this section, and its companion italic Univers 56.

The Univers numbering system is an interesting innovation. It dispenses with the vague "bold/light/condensed/extended" terminology we have saddled ourselves with for so long. The two digits indicate precisely where the variants fit in the spectrum. The lower numbers are the lighter faces; odd numbers are roman, even numbers italic; high second digits identify more condensed faces. Univers 55 is just about the middle of the palette.

84

abcdefghijklmnopqrstuvwxyz
ABCDEFGHIJKLMNOPQRSTUVWXYZ
1234567890(.,:;!?"—/$-%)

abcdefghijklmnopqrstuvwxyz
ABCDEFGHIJKLMNOPQRSTUVWXYZ
1234567890(.,:;!?"—/$-%)

Univers is also known as Alphavers, Aries, Boston, Galaxy, UN, Unistar, and Versatile.

The even-width monoweights are not merely more versatile than their uneven-width cousins; they are also, as a rule, less stringently geometric. The thinning and thickening for optical uniformity is not as meticulously controlled, and the bolder faces are quite obviously shaded. The x-heights are also considerably larger, so the even-widths are preferable as text faces. The small variations add a touch of warmth to this branch of the family that was deliberately avoided in Futura. The Bauhaus might not have approved, but the more humanistic letterforms seem in keeping with contemporary taste, and probably explain the success of these typefaces.

Here are some more of them.

abcdefghijklmnopqrstuvwxyz
ABCDEFGHIJKLMNOPQRSTUVWXYZ

c e w y A A N N

A newer member of the even-width family, Avant

85

Garde was designed in 1962 for *Avant-Garde Magazine* by the late Herb Lubalin, one of the most versatile of American designers (he was also responsible for the famous PBS logotype). It is a fairly light, open, round face with a calligraphic touch. Perhaps its most unusual feature is the set of supplementary kerning characters, some of which are shown. It was used ad nauseam in the 1970s, and has since declined in favor. Once the fad is forgotten, however, it should take its proper place as one of the most attractive evenwidths.

abcdefghijklmnopqrstuvwxyz
ABCDEFGHIJKLMNOPQRSTUVWXYZ

Folio, which was designed in 1957 by Konrad Bauer and Walter Baum (many recent sans serifs are team efforts), is closest to the early nineteenth-century sans serifs, which were all even-widths. It is an open, medium-weight face with well-differentiated shading.

abcdefghijklmnopqrstuvwxyz
ABCDEFGHIJKLMNOPQRSTUVWXYZ

Franklin Gothic, another Morris Benton design, might be considered the last of the nineteenth century "gothics" although it appeared in the first decade of this century. It is a plain, no-nonsense face, with something of the utilitarian style of Futura, although it is an even-width. It is also the heaviest of the standard monoweights; its regular fonts are as heavy as some boldfaces. Despite its age, however, it is a serviceable face and still popular.

abcdefghijklmnopqrstuvwxyz
ABCDEFGHIJKLMNOPQRSTUVWXYZ

Helvetica was another 1957 face—a banner year for

sans serifs—by the Swiss designer Max Miedinger. It was one of the most popular faces of the Sixties, but was then temporarily supplanted by Univers. More recently it has made a major comeback. It is a heavier face than Folio, more geometric than Univers, and remains one of the most useful of the even-widths, as its many pseudonyms attest. (Also Claro, Corvus, Geneva, HE, Helios, Megaron, New Haas Grotesk—its original name—Newton, Vega)

abcdefghijklmnopqrstuvwxyz
ABCDEFGHIJKLMNOPQRSTUVWXYZ

News Gothic is an old warhorse, produced in 1908 by the prolific Morris Benton. It is a light, narrow, utilitarian face designed originally as a newspaper face. It went through a major revival in the 1950s, when a whole slew of new weights were added. (Also Alpha Gothic, Classified News Medium, Gothstar Trade, Toledo, Trade Gothic)

abcdefghijklmnopqrstuvwxyz
ABCDEFGHIJKLMNOPQRSTUVWXYZ

Standard is well-named because it is the oldest of the modern sans serifs and set the style for the later even-widths; it first appeared in 1896 and is still going strong. It is a plain, open face, lighter than most even-widths, and with a comfortably large x-height. It is an excellent text face. (Also Akzidenz Grotesk, its original name)

Shaded Sans Serifs

The monoweights, by and large, have dominated type design since the 1950s, but another branch of the family, the shaded sans serifs, has steadily been gaining ground.

They are far easier to distinguish than the monoweights because they are infinitely more diverse in appearance.

87

There are both even-width and uneven-width faces, but they are all two-weight alphabets. In a sense, they represent something of a revolt against the strictness of mono-weight design. At the same time, they are very much contemporary in style.

A typical shaded is yet another Zapf face, Optima, which was published a year later than Univers. This section is set in Optima.

abcdefghijklmnopqrstuvwxyz
ABCDEFGHIJKLMNOPQRSTUVWXYZ
1234567890(.,:;!?" —/$-%)

abcdefghijklmnopqrstuvwxyz
ABCDEFGHIJKLMNOPQRSTUVWXYZ
1234567890(.,:;!?"—/$-%)

Zapf designed Optima primarily as a text face, an unusual departure for sans serifs. Like most of his designs, it has a strongly calligraphic feeling. In fact, it also has oldstyle proportions and an almost Venetian old style shading, with the typical splayed M and lower-case g. At the same time, Optima is a clean-cut, strictly contemporary face. In a sense, Zapf had the best of both worlds, and this freedom may well be the chief attraction of the shaded sans serifs to designers and readers alike. Certainly, Optima is one of the most popular faces around. (Also Chelmsford, Musica, OP, Optimist, Optistar, Oracle, Orleans, Theme, Ursa, Zenith.)

Here is a sampling of other shadeds to illustrate the range of this branch of the family.

88

abcdefghijklmnopqrstuvwxyz
ABCDEFGHIJKLMNOPQRSTUVWXYZ

Ad Lib is a slightly nutty 1961 jeu d'esprit by Freeman Craw, who cut out the original letterforms instead of drawing them. The resulting rough-edged shapes in no way detract from the readability of the face. There are alternative versions of many of the characters, which can be supplemented by reversing the standard forms (b/d, n/u and so on). Despite its obvious eccentricities, Ad Lib is a highly legible face, even for text.

abcdefghijklmnopqrstuvwxyz
ABCDEFGHIJKLMNOPQRSTUVWXYZ

Britannic is an English shaded in the fat-face tradition. It is typical of a group of faces that were popular in the 1930s and are now associated strongly with the theater and motion pictures. Several other fat-faced shadeds have also appeared in the last few years. Obviously, they are purely display types.

abcdefghijklmnopqrstuvwxyz
ABCDEFGHIJKLMNOPQRSTUVWXYZ

Eras is a fairly recent addition to the family. It was designed by Albert Boton and introduced by the International Typeface Company in 1976. The design is quite unusual with its forward leaning characters and unjoined loops (such as the lower-case a). It is also unusually wide-setting for a sans serif. Despite its eccentricities, however, it is an exceptionally readable text face, a striking display face, and promises to be one of the vogue types of the eighties. The heads in this book are set in Eras Demi and Eras Light.

abcdefghijklmnopqrstuvwxyz
ABCDEFGHIJKLMNOPQRSTUVWXYZ

Friz Quadrata was designed by the Swiss Ernst Friz and

issued in a full range of variants by ITC in the early 1970s. It might be classified as a Latin face or copperplate gothic because of its minute triangular serifs, but it is distinctly a contemporary sans serif in style. The characters are crisply cut and the intrusive white space created by the unclosed loops give it a additional sparkle. The upper case is clearly based on Trajanic caps. Despite its obvious eccentricities, the large x-height and legible letterforms make this an excellent text type as well as an effective display face.

ABCDEFGHIJKLMNOPQRSTUVWXYZ

Microgramma is another team effort, by the Italian designers Alessandro Butti and Aldo Novarese. It is a distinctly unusual design, with extended, rectangular letterforms and only the slightest degree of shading. It has no lower case, but Novarese produced Eurostile, a virtually identical, but lighter, face with a lower case some years later. If at first you don't succeed . . . (Also ES, Eurogothic, Europa, Eurostyle(!), Microstyle, and Waltham).

ABCDEFGHIJKLMNOPQRS
TUVWXYZ

Neuland is another Rudolf Koch design, from 1923, but is a far cry from Kabel. It seems to have been carved from rock by a Neanderthal (in fact, Koch is reputed to have cut it freehand). The weighting and letterforms are irregular and slabby, but, while not exactly your everyday face, Neuland is eye-catching and nowhere near as crude as it seems at first acquaintance. There is no lower case, and I am not sure that one could be designed.

abcdefghijklmnopqrstuvwxyz
ABCDEFGHIJKLMNOPQRSTUVWXYZ

Peignot, a 1937 design by A. M. Cassandre, is an even

more eccentric face. Its most striking peculiarity is the mixture of upper-case forms in the lower case. The contrast of shading is marked, although the thins are fairly heavy. The letterforms range from the conventional to the whimsical, and are an irregular mélange of sharply cut shapes, needle-like points and slack curves, typical of late-Thirties design. Despite its idiosyncracies, Peignot has become a popular face, perhaps because it reflects the confused eighties. (Also Penyoe.)

DECORATIVES

The issue of readability has rarely plagued the designers of decoratives, and they have cropped up in every period of type design. These are not, and are not generally intended to be, text faces—and that may be the only feature they have in common. Some designers refer to them as the "hell box" which was once the receptacle kept in the corner of the type shop for broken type.

It is almost impossible to catalog these faces logically; they cut across all other type families. However, I have tried to make sense out of this motley collection, which ranges from the sublime to the ridiculous, by first dividing them into two broad groups and subdividing these into more comprehensible compartments.

The first group I have called "imitatives" because they mimic non-typographic forms. The second, which have some pretensions to being legitimate typefaces, I have called "typographic".

There really isn't much that can be said about the use of decoratives that isn't self-evident, except a general warning to stay away from them as much as possible.

Imitatives

It is not entirely clear why anybody would want to design a typeface that looked like script (except to avoid the expense of hand-lettering) or typewriter type, but this group is quite common among the decoratives.

I have divided them into two broad categories; scripts, which imitate handwritten form, and nonscripts (which might better be called nondescripts) that resemble some other alphanumeric form.

Scripts   This group includes types that resemble virtually every hand-written style.

abcdefghijklmnopqrstuvwxyz
ABCDEFGHIJKLMNOPQRSTUVWXYZ

Cloister Black is typical of a number of blackletter faces, and a trifle more readable than most. It is inevitably connected with things ecclesiastical, academic, and legal. Oddly enough, a considerable number of newspaper nameplates are set in blackletter.

abcdefghijklmnopqrstuvwxyz

Libra is a cleanly cut face by S. H. De Roos, based on uncial script. There is no upper case.

Aa Bb Cc Dd Ee Ff Gg Hh Ii Jj Kk Ll Mm
Nn Oo Pp Qq Rr Ss Tt Uu Vv Ww Xx Yy Zz

Kuenstler Bold Script is a typical copperplate, inevitably associated with formal occasions—White House and weddings, Cartier and Cadillacs. Like all copperplates, it is virtually unreadable.

abcdefghijklmnopqrstuvwxyz
ABCDEFGHIJKLMNOPQRSTUVWXYZ

Lydian is a masterly display of broad-pen calligraphy by another leading American designer, Warren Chappell. It is a bold, clean-cut face that might almost be included with the shaded sans serifs.

abcdefghijklmnopqrstuvwxyz
ABCDEFGHIJKLMNOPQRSTUVWXYZ

Zapf Chancery is a less formal italic by the master.

92

Aa Bb Cc Dd Ee Ff Gg Hh Ji Jj Kk Ll
Mm Nn Oo Pp Qq Rr Ss Tt Uu Vv Ww Xx

Present is an informal, almost casual, pen script that might have been dashed off with a broad-tipped marker.

ABCDEFGHIJKLMNOPQRSTUVWXYZ

Balloon Bold is a popular brush face, saved from rigidity by the unclosed junctions of the main strokes. There is an authoritative Extra Bold, but no lower case for either version.

abcdefghijklmnopqrstuvwxyz
ABCDEFGHIJKLMNOPQRSTUVWXYZ

Mistral is an informal brush face that has become a favorite of advertising designers. The caps are crisply drawn, but the lower case, which has links to simulate hand-lettering, seems too small for them and is not particularly readable. However, the same holds true for most informal brush faces.

Like the script decoratives, the nonscripts emulate untypographic alphabets.

Nonscripts

abcdefghijklmnopqrstuvwxyz
ABCDEFGHIJKLMNOPQRSTUVWXYZ

American Typewriter is one of several typewriter faces. They represent the ultimate absurdity in type design.

abcdefghijklmnopqrstuvwxyz
ABCDEFGHIJKLMNOPQRSTUVWXYZ

Amelia is a "computer" face, and perhaps readable only to a

computer. There are other digital faces resembling LED read-outs and optical character recognition types.

ABCDEFGHIJKLMNOPQRSTUVWXYZ

Stencil is meant to look like the kind of lettering painted onto packing cases, crates, tea chests and government property. It is a favorite of junk mailers and lottery promoters.

Typographics   The typographic decoratives are generally easier to take than the imitatives. In fact, there are a number of excellent designs, including some classic faces, among their number. They are a variegated collection, but I have divided them into six sub-categories for convenience: titling faces, inlines and outlines, shadowed faces, ornamented faces, decorative faces, and novelties.

Titling faces   Titling faces are generally based on Roman square capitals, and more particularly the superb letters on the base of Trajan's column, which have inspired many calligraphers and type designers. Several standard faces, such as Times Roman and Gill Sans, have titling versions. These two examples, however, were designed purely as titling faces.

ABCDEFGHIJKLMNOPQR STUVWXYZ

Augustea is another design by the Butti and Novarese team. It follows the Trajanic original closely.

ABCDEFGHIJKKLMNOPQ QRRSSTUVWXYZ

Michaelangelo, another Zapf face, was also inspired by the

94

Trajanic caps, but is much lighter and more calligraphic than Augustea.

Technically, an inline is a narrow stripe running through the main stroke of a letter. If it runs along one edge, it is sometimes referred to as shading (just to confuse things), although some typographers use the same term for a series of inlines producing a cross-hatched effect. A broad inline is called chiseling. For simplicity's sake, I've called the whole kit and caboodle inlines. Outlines is self-explanatory. Many standard faces have inline and outline fonts.

Inlines and outlines

ABCDEFGHIJKLMNOP QRSTUVWXYZabcdefg hijklmnopqrstuvwxyz

Astoria's inline forms a narrow rim around the letters, a style popular in the nineteenth century. The hairline border tends to blur or break if it is not printed meticulously.

abcdefghijklmnopqrstuvwxyz
ABCDEFGHIJKLMNOPQRSTUVW

Broadway Engraved has a single inline running through the thick strokes. It is a variant of a fat-face shaded sans serif popular in the 1930s, and was originally called Boul Mich, a name that conjures up the expatriate American artists who descended on Paris's Left Bank around that time.

ABCDEFGHIJKLMNOPQ
RSTUVWXYZ

De Roos Inline is an elegant, calligraphic, even-width set of

Trajanic caps with a tapered inline running through the center of the thick strokes. This adds brilliance without impairing readability.

ABCDEFGHIJKLMNOPQRSTU
VWXYZ

Prisma is a triple-inline version of Kabel. It has the solidity of the original but the inlines give it a light appearance. Highly readable as a display face, it tends—like all multiple inlines— to become dazzling and uncomfortably stroboscopic in very large sizes.

abcdefghijklmnopqrstuvwxyz
ABCDEFGHIJKLMNOPQRSTUVWXYZ

Many standard faces have outline variants; this is the outline version of Americana. All outline faces should be printed on smooth papers, if at all.

Shadowed faces Almost everyone has created a shadowed face, usually on the back cover of an algebra text. Type designers are essentially human beings, but they get paid for doing the same thing. They have created a galaxy of faces with a simulated third dimension. Strangely, shadowing almost universally appears on the right side of the letters.

abcdefghijklmnopqrstuvwxyz
ABCDEFGHIJKLMNOPQRSTUVWXYZ

Chisel is a Latin face—that is, it has triangular serifs—with a small shadow on the right. It was issued by the English type-founders Stephenson Blake in 1939, but is reminiscent of a style very popular in the Victorian era.

ABCDEFGHIJKLMNO PQRSTUVWXYZ

Thorne Shaded is a classic face, with a full third dimension, but no attempt at perspective. It appeared in 1820, but is not the oldest of the tribe. That distinction belongs to Figgins' Shaded which appeared in the same year as Caslon's abortive two-line Egyptian; Figgins went on to publish the second sans serif in 1832. Full-dimension shadows are generally not drawn in perspective because there would be no common vanishing point for the characters when they were set in a line. The effect would be not only incongruous, but visually disturbing, and letterspacing would be almost impossible.

ABCDEFGHIJKLMNOPQR STUVWXYZ

Augustea Shaded is a shadowed version of the titling face. The shadow is internal, creating the illusion that the characters are incised in stone. Several standard faces have similar shaded or incised variants.

ABCDEFGHIJKLMNOPQRST UVWXYZ

Gold Nugget is a heavy square serif with solid characters and a reversed shadow, rendered in outline. This treatment is relatively uncommon, probably because it tends to make the type look slightly jittery.

In this group, some form of decorative pattern or device is imposed on the characters, although the letterforms themselves are generally not altered.

Decorated faces

97

ABCDEFGHIJKLMNOP
QRSTUVWXYZ

Fry's Ornamented is a venerable decorated (I don't care if it is called Ornamented), designed by Richard Austin, a contemporary of Baskerville. The basic design is a hybrid transitional/ modern with an inline. Despite the decoration, it is a crisp, elegant and readable face.

ABCDEFGHIJKLMNO
PQRSTUVWXYZ

Saphir is a modern fat face with a calligraphic quality. It is bold and delicate at the same time. It was designed by Gudrun Zapf von Hesse, one of the small but growing band of female designers.

ABCDEFGHIJKLMNOPQRSTUVWXYZ

American Antique, like too many decorated faces, goes a little too far. It is, in fact, both ornamented and decorated; one or the other is usually enough. It might come in handy if you are designing a circus banner or a calliope, but I can't think of any other use for it off-hand.

Ornamented faces   In this group, the decorative effect is achieved by manipulating the letterforms. The results are often interesting, sometimes striking, and usually unreadable.

abcdefghijklmnopqrstuvwxyz
ABCDEFGHIJKLMNOPQRSTUVWXYZ

Arnold Böcklin is a curlicued reverse-weight, vaguely reminiscent of the Lombardic capitals sometimes used as initials for

98

blackletter manuscripts. It is typical of many Art Nouveau faces, which seem to be making a comeback along with Tiffany lamp-shades and Beardsley drawings. They are often charming in effect but rarely readable.

abcdefghijklmnopqrstuvwxyz
ABCDEFGHIJKLMNOPQRSTUVWXYZ

Fantail is a decorative reverse-weight. Decoratives, reverse-weight and otherwise, were a Victorian passion; so were fret-work, architectural gingerbread, antimacassars, bustles and chairs made of buffalo horns. Few of them were visually pleasing or served any useful purpose.

ABCDEFGIJKLMNP
QRSTUVWXYZ

Gallia is a curlicued fat face with a double inline. Despite my earlier comment, it is surprisingly readable, even in relatively small sizes. Again, however, the hairlines need a smooth paper and meticulous printing.

ABCDEFGIJKLM
NPQRSTUVXYZ

Thunderbird is a big, brash face that conjures up the Old West. Faces with spiked strokes like this are sometimes called Tuscans, for reasons that escape me. Tuscany is a region north of Rome, famous for Dante, the Etruscans, and straw hats.

abcdefghijklmnopqrstuvwxyz
ABCDEFGHIJKLMNOPQRSTUVWXYZ

Hobo is a cheerful, cartoon-like sans serif by Morris Benton, with descenders tucked up above the baseline. Not exactly a classic design, but it is readable and distinctive.

Novelties
This last category is reserved for the more bizarre flights of fantasy. There is no other rationale for the group, and almost no practical reason to use any of them.*

abcdefghijklmnopqrstuvwxyz
ABCDEFGHIJKLMNOPQRSTUVWXYZ

abcdefghijklmnopqrstuvwxyz
ABCDEFGHIJKLMNOPQRSTUVWXYZ

abcdefghijklmnopqrstuvwxyz
ABCDEFGHIJKLMNOPQRSTUVW

ABCDEFGHIJKLMNOPQRST

ABCDEFGHIJKLMNOPQRSTUVWXYZ

ABCDEFGHIJKLMNOPQRSTUVWXYZ

ABCDEFGHIJK
LMNOPQRSTUV

abcdefghijklmnopqrstuvwxyz
ABCDEFGHIJKLMNOPQRSTUVWXYZ

ABCDEFGHIJKLMNOPQRSTUVWXYZ

This last typeface is called Stop, which, in the circumstances, seems like good advice.

*Purely for the record, they are—in order—Devendra, Pierrot, Rainbow Bass, Ben Franklin Initials, Neon, Hebrastyle, Raffia, Lilith, and Stop.

4 TYPE TECHNIQUE

Many of the students in my design course start with a plaintive "But I can't draw." Neither can many working designers.

Type design is not creative in the same sense as painting, sculpture, or, for that matter, needlepoint or ceramics. You can produce perfectly respectable designs without the lofty imagination that creates Sistine Chapel ceilings, although you may never stand in the first rank of typographers. Obviously, you must have some degree of visual imagination, and graphic skills are a distinct asset, but you will never be a successful designer without the more mundane ability to find logical solutions to design problems.

Design is a whole brain process. It draws on the logical, verbal, mathematical, left hemisphere as much as the intuitive, visual, right hemisphere. You could produce a design purely by intuition, but I doubt if it would be aimed at the reader. You might equally produce a design purely on mechanical principles, but it would probably appeal to nobody.

Type designers are closer to architects than to artists. The architect must produce a building that is structurally sound and efficient but that is also visually pleasing and comfortable to live and work in. Consequently, he or she must know as much about the physical properties of building materials, wind pressure, sheer and stress, and the dimensions of heating ducts as about the esthetics of three-dimensional space and the psychology of color.

The type designer similarly must combine a strong visual imagination with a sound knowledge of psychology, the physiology of the human eye, and the complexities of typesetting and print technology. But, unlike the architect, who can order up whatever building materials he or she wants, the designer's basic material is usually pre-selected by somebody else—the writer or editor. So the designer must also have a flair for analysis and interpretation and considerable skill in human relations.

The designer, then, is a jack/jill-of-all-trades. But when all is said and done, good design is largely a matter of good sense; of perspiration rather than inspiration. You always start with two eminently practical questions: Who are we trying to communicate with? and What are we trying to tell them? You can then answer the critical design question: How do we do it?

There are designers who see design as an end in itself. They produce 'pure' design or simply impose the same old boilerplate on every job. Or, perhaps worse still, they reproduce whatever happens to be trendy at the moment. Or they are doctrinaires— the reactionaries who never use sans serifs for text and think asymmetrical layouts should be outlawed, or the radicals who never use anything else and think justified setting should be banned by law. They often win design awards.

Their counterparts are the writers and editors who regard design as an irrelevant frill. But design is as integral to the print medium as words. Words are the substance; design is the form. Neither can communicate effectively without the other, and it is the synergy of well-written words and well-conceived design that makes print work.

If a design is unappealing, the readers may never be tempted to read a word. If it is inappropriate, they will approach the content with a false impression that will be difficult to correct. And that impression is formed instantaneously. The design is the first thing that meets the readers' eyes and colors their immediate response to the product, even if subliminally.

The contradictory challenge facing every designer is to produce a physical form for the words that is at once appealing and unobtrusive, or 'transparent' to use the designer's term. If reading is to be effortless, the reader must be almost (or completely) unaware of the design.

You won't conjure up a transparent design by sinking into a trance and waiting for inspired celestial voices to speak. Plan-

Identical text, but very different first impressions. The upper version might have been taken from an entomological handbook.

BEST PRINTING
TRADITION

The best printing follows traditional lines because printing is a conservative as well as preservative art, and these lines are the result of innumerable efforts in the past to produce the best, conditioned by the materials at hand and the capabilities of the producer himself.

All the crafts—the mechanical arts, and especially printing—are subject to different standards of criticism from those used to evaluate a work of fine art—of painting, music, sculpture; because fine art, if it has no pleasure or meaning for the observer, may be merely passed by or ignored. You don't have to look at a picture.

BOOKS MORE THAN
AN ASSEMBLAGE

But books are more than just an assemblage of types and paper to be looked at; they are also texts, and it is desirable and necessary to get at the text, regardless of the physical form in which it is presented. It follows then that no matter what style the design of a book conforms to; it must be one that presents the text clearly, without distractions of queer composition, odd types, or meaningless decoration.

The best printing follows traditional lines because printing is a conservative as well as preservative art, and these lines are the result of innumerable efforts in the past to produce the best, conditioned by the materials at hand and the capabilities of the producer himself. All the crafts—the mechanical arts, and especially printing—are subject to different standards of criticism from those used to evaluate a work of fine art—of painting, music, sculpture; because fine art, if it has no pleasure or meaning for the observer, may be merely passed by or ignored. You don't have to look at a picture.

But books are more than just an assemblage of types and paper to be looked at; they are also texts, and it is desirable and necessary to get at the text, regardless of the physical form in which it is presented. It follows then that no matter what style the design of a book conforms to; it must be one that presents the text clearly, without distractions of queer composition, odd types, or meaningless decoration.

ning your design takes careful, conscious thought—plus a modicum of inspiration—and that is where the perspiration comes in.

PLANNING THE DESIGN

Planning a design is fundamentally a matter of finding sensible answers to "who?", "what?", and "how?".

The most practical way to start is to tackle the "what?" first, by reading your manuscript thoroughly, completely and intelligently, whether it is five lines of advertising copy or five hundred pages of book text. You must be completely familiar with the content, but you must also be sensitive to the tone and style of the writing. All three must be reflected in your design.

At the same time, a thorough reading immediately eliminates many unproductive approaches. For instance, if the copy is written with a light, informal touch, you will probably not want to set it in solid slabs of businesslike sans serifs. If it is strictly factual and written in a serious, sober style, you can forget about decorative heads and unconventional layouts.

You will also have a clear idea of the amount of material you have to deal with, and the number of individual type and graphic components.

Ideally, design should be considered from the inception of the product. It seldom is. The physical specifications are usually based on cost, and the length of the copy on content. Designers rarely have anything to say about either and can even more rarely persuade anyone to change them after the event. And you will discover that there is a widespread belief among non-designers that any given amount of copy can be fitted into any given space. Pointing out that 30 pages of manuscript and sixteen photographs can't be shoehorned comfortably into a 16-page booklet with a 7″ × 9″ trim will usually be met with a blank expression.

Nevertheless, virtually every design decision you make will depend on the relationship between the amount of copy and the space available to print it. You must know what that relationship is before you go any farther.

The next logical step, then, is to cast off, or estimate the length of, your copy. (Several methods are described in Appendix A.)

If you are working with copy set on a word-processor, the job may have been done for you. Many word-processors count keystrokes (that is, characters). If not, it is fairly simple to cast off by finding out the capacity of the disks and the percentage taken up by the copy. Even the most primitive word-processing systems will provide this information. If you are working with old-fashioned hard copy, pounded out on a typewriter, you will simply have to knuckle down and do some old-fashioned mathematics.

With the cast-off, you have really answered the "what?". You now know the message to be transmitted and the style of the message, the amount of copy and the number and frequency of the typographic components, such as heads, and the number and style of the graphic elements, if any.

The next order of business is "Who is the reader?".

It is a mistake to think about readers-in-the-plural. If you do, you will almost certainly wind up designing for a stereotype or a statistical average instead of a human being. Average readers are about as common as average hens' teeth. Reading is a solitary occupation, and, even though your design may eventually reach thousands of readers, every one will be reading alone in a particular place at a particular time.

You design for that particular individual.

Perhaps the best way to bring the individual reader alive is to write his or her (imaginary) biography. Writers often use this technique, but, in my experience, few designers do. However, the mere fact of writing seems to imprint the reader's image more firmly on your mind, perhaps because it forces you to dig out detailed information that might otherwise be overlooked.

Not all of the information may be cogent, but you need to know at least your reader's gender, age, occupation, social background, education, religion, politics, hobbies and interests, passions and prejudices. Is he or she (and is that a significant point?) an urbanite, a suburbanite or plain country folk? A Yankee, a Southerner, a Sunbelter, or a laid-back Californian? One of a fairly homogeneous group, such as a member of a church congregation or a devotee of three-dimensional chess, or of a heterogeneous crowd, such as an Amtrak passenger, an IBM stockholder, or a dues-paying Republican? You should know.

Bishops, brokers, bartenders and Boy Scouts are not likely to respond to the same design in the same way.

Once you have the answers, you have added the "who?" to the "what?" and you can begin to make some rational decisions about the form of your design. For example, if your reader is over fifty, he or she has probably reached the Bifocal Age and will not enjoy struggling with 9-point type—even if the bifocals have not been left in the glove compartment. The same applies to teachers, who are as short-sighted as the rest of the population but are notoriously averse to wearing glasses, particularly in the classroom.

You should also be able to make an intelligent estimate of your reader's level of motivation. Some things are read for pleasure or interest; some because they are unavoidable. Subscribers to a ski magazine or an investment newsletter are motivated readers by definition—people don't pay for publications they don't want to read. On the other hand, the reader of an in-house magazine or an employee newsletter may not be as highly motivated. Readers of advertising or promotional blurbs may be considered neutral or indifferent (at least to start with). Readers of textbooks, traffic tickets, insurance policies and tax instructions can be regarded as reluctant, at best. With a highly motivated reader, you can usually concentrate on readability; with a reluctant reader, you may have to concentrate on appeal, even at the expense of readability.

Finally, you should think about where and when the product will be used. Books, brochures, posters and bumper stickers will probably be seen in adequate light. Highway signs, on the other hand, must be designed for high visibility at night. A menu may have to be read in the light of a single candle; the prices must still be readable. And the instructions for changing a tire have to be visible by the light of a fading flashlight in a rainstorm on the outskirts of Slapout, Oklahoma. Circumstances alter cases, or, in this instance, faces.

By this stage, the "how?" should be taking shape although you have been planning primarily with your left brain. At worst, you have eliminated profitless approaches, and narrowed down useful approaches for your right brain to explore. The purely conceptual phase of planning is complete, and it is time to convert the concept into a concrete design scheme. This is the point where your right brain must take over.

Your first attempts to give shape to the design are thumbnails. Thumbnailing is sometimes called "noodling", but I have always objected to the term because it implies fiddling around and hoping for the pieces to fall into place. The professional designer thumbnails with a purpose, shaping a fairly well-defined idea by controlled trial-and-error, which is pretty much the way the right brain operates.

Thumbnails are experiments aimed at producing the basic pattern of the design, without worrying too much about specifics. In effect, you are creating the instantaneous impression that the readers receive when they first see the product.

I generally thumbnail with a broad sketching pencil or felt-tip marker to prevent myself from becoming too finicky too early. At this stage, you should be looking only for a general balance of the major typographic and graphic components. Another widely used technique is to rough out each of these elements, cut them out, and treat them like the pieces of a jigsaw. Some elements will fall into place fairly quickly; others will not, and can be discarded and replaced with variations until the right combination emerges.

Sometimes, you will be afflicted with the designer's equivalent of 'writer's block'. Nothing works and you seem to be going nowhere. Essentially, your right brain is telling you that you are on the wrong track and it needs time to mull over the problem; it may be inarticulate, but it is not dumb. Intuitive thinking cannot be forced no matter how well you have laid the groundwork of logic. The remedy is to walk away from the problem, even if only for the time it takes to brew a cup of coffee. The chances are that the answer will suddenly occur to you about a minute after you get back to the drawing board.

Eventually, no matter what approach you take, you will arrive by successive approximations at a satisfactory sketch. You may decide to work it up in more detail, but essentially you are through with planning. The last step is to scale up your thumbnail to a precise, actual-size layout and begin to work on the specifics of the design.

EXECUTING THE DESIGN

It would take a broader vision—and more gall—than I possess to suggest guidelines for an appealing design. Esthetics are not yet definable, and taste is largely a personal matter. There are no sure-fire formulas for either.

There are, however, some well-tried techniques for creating a readable design.

Readability, whatever the editors of Webster's may think, is not the same as legibility to a designer. Legibility is inherent in the design of the characters. The poet Robert Bridges defined it very succinctly as "the certainty of decipherment". In other words, legibility is a measure of the clarity of the letter-forms. In essence, the closer the design to the fundamental shapes of the alphabet, the more legible it is likely to be. Decoratives by their very nature are generally the least legible faces because their characters have been deliberately distorted in some way. Some of the more extreme examples are just plain illegible. Text faces, such as Caslon and Optima, are generally legible in any context.

Most standard typefaces, like Caslon, Century Schoolbook and Univers at top, are highly legible even when the words are unfamiliar, but you would have a hard time getting to Xochimilco if the highway signs were in an illegible face such as the Commercial Script at bottom.

ATZCAPOTZALCO

TEXCALTITLAN

KANTUNILKIN

MIXQUIAHUALA

COSAMALOAPAN

XOCHIMILCO

As a designer, there isn't a great deal you can do about the legibility of a face; but you can do a great deal about the readability of the type. Readability in the designer's sense might be described as that aspect of the design that makes the type comfortable to read.

The subject has become something of a playground for researchers. About 3,000 studies on readability have been published in the last few decades, but most of them are of only peripheral value to the working designer. Many are too arcane, too specific or too contradictory for practical application. On the whole, however, research results tend to validate the more-intuitive principles followed by typographers from time immemorial.

I am not decrying research, but until a more coherent and practical body of results develops, there is no good reason to abandon well-established practice.

As far as the designer is concerned, readability is the result of a complex balance of factors (and it may be the complexity that frustrates researchers and fascinates designers). The inherent legibility of the typeface is obviously one factor, but type size, style and weight, line length, spacing, setting, and format are equally important considerations. For example, Century Schoolbook is a highly legible face, but it is not exactly readable in 4-point italics nor, at the normal reading distance of 15–18 inches, in 72-point bold caps. On the other hand, 12-point Century Schoolbook, which would be a highly readable text type, would not be readable on a poster with a normal viewing distance of 6 feet or more.

To create a readable design, you have to arrive at an appropriate balance of these factors for the context in which the design is to function.

Type Size

Broadly speaking, large type sizes are more readable than small type sizes—with some critical qualifications.

The old rule of thumb is that up to 14 points you see the words and over 16 points you see the letters. There is still no satisfactory explanation of the phenomenon, but the empirical evidence is fairly convincing; 14 points is the practical limit for text faces.

Even so, we have to be careful about the term 'size'. In any given typeface, the 12 point fonts will be more readable than the equivalent 8 point fonts, but the 12 point fonts of different faces are not equally readable. Some typefaces appear to be larger than others of the same nominal size; in fact, they may look larger than other faces in a higher point size. Here is an example:

Printing is fundamentally a selection of materials already in existence, and an assembling of these different varieties of types and papers and ornaments; and it is the way that they are assembled that counts in the effect. One can take almost any kind of type and produce extremely varied	Printing is fundamentally a selection of materials already in existence, and an assembling of these different varieties of types and papers and ornaments; and it is the way that they are assembled that counts in the effect. One can take almost any kind of type and produce extremely varied results by different methods

The paragraph on the left is set in 11 point Bodoni; the paragraph on the right is in 10 point Optima. The Optima looks larger than the Bodoni although it is nominally one point size smaller.

The critical factor is the difference in x-height.

Nominal point size refers to the height of the shoulder of the type, not the size of the printed image. In fact, you can't calculate the point size from the printed image. In the first place, some space was left on the shoulder of the type below the descender so that it would not touch the ascenders in the line below. In the second, the sides of the raised printing area were beveled for strength to withstand the force of the press, so the face of the type is automatically offset from the sides.

However, within the limits of the shoulder, the designer of the face can arrange the proportions of the lower-case letters as he or she chooses.

Bodoni followed the contemporary fashion for long ascenders and descenders; consequently, he had to settle for a low x-height. Zapf, who designed Optima, decided on a large x-height, leaving only a limited amount of room for the ascenders and descenders. However, the x-height components in a mass of type far outweigh the skinny ascenders and descenders.

Moreover, when the descenders are short, the baseline is lower on the shoulder and the caps are correspondingly larger.

11pt **Hjbx⸺xbjH** *10pt*

Long ascenders and descenders also "trap" far more white space inside the word-shape, which squeezes the x-height characters optically, making them look smaller than they are. As a result, large x-height faces create an optical illusion of size that has little to do with the nominal size of the type.

Consequently, point size is a deceptive indicator. It simply tells you the depth of the line. If you look at the two paragraphs again, you will see that although both are 110 points deep, there are 11 lines of Optima to the 10 lines of the smaller-looking Bodoni.

For the designer, then, x-height is the critical factor in judging the size of a typeface. The problem for a new designer is that typefaces are not specified by x-height, and it takes some time and experience to sort them out. As a general rule, however, more recent designs tend to have more generous x-heights than older faces. In the oldstyles, for example, x-heights are usually between 55 percent and 60 percent of the cap size; in the sans serifs, they are more likely to be about 70 percent of the cap size. In Appendix B, I have listed some common faces in increasing order of x-height to get you started.

The same problem applies to width. Alphabet lengths have never been standardized. However, the width, or set, of a typeface is important for two reasons. First, from a purely practical point of view, the set dictates the number of characters that will fit into a line, which is a critical factor in copyfitting. Second, set influences readability because, generally, the wider the set, the more readable the type.

The lack of a uniform standard makes it difficult to compare the set of different faces. However, the length of the lower-case alphabet is a fairly accurate guide. This measure was normally supplied in hot metal specimen books. More recently, it seems to have been dropped, presumably because the ability to letter-space at will makes the idea of "normal" set meaningless.

Another guide is the characters-per-pica counts or character-count tables supplied by your typesetter. These are slightly cruder measures because they are averages, taken from thousands of lines of type, without regard for variations in word-spacing (which could skew the results). However, for that reason, they may be more realistic for text faces, although they are a shaky guide for display.

Set varies considerably more than x-height within type families and from one family to another, so each face has to be judged on its own merits. Here is a sampling of standard faces which illustrates the inconsistency:

abcdefghijklmnopqrstuvwxyz
abcdefghijklmnopqrstuvwxyz
abcdefghijklmnopqrstuvwxyz
abcdefghijklmnopqrstuvwxyz
abcdefghijklmnopqrstuvwxyz
abcdefghijklmnopqrstuvwxyz
abcdefghijklmnopqrstuvwxyz
abcdefghijklmnopqrstuvwxyz
abcdefghijklmnopqrstuvwxyz
abcdefghijklmnopqrstuvwxyz
abcdefghijklmnopqrstuvwxyz
abcdefghijklmnopqrstuvwxyz

Even fonts of the same face in the same point size may vary unpredictably in set. Here are four 12 point fonts of Goudy Old Style:

abcdefghijklmnopqrstuvwxyz
abcdefghijklmnopqrstuvwxyz
abcdefghijklmnopqrstuvwxyz
abcdefghijklmnopqrstuvwxyz

Even more depressingly, cuts of the same face by different manufacturers are likely to have different sets.

Again, time and experience will give you a feeling for the set of different faces. In the interim, you can always compare sample fonts directly, or consult Appendix C where there is a selection of standard faces arranged in increasing order of alphabet length.

As far as displays are concerned, vertical or horizontal size is not a critical factor because the reader is more likely to piece them out letter by letter, rather than by word-shape.

Type Style

By the x-height criterion, Optima is more readable than Bodoni. However, some designers—and researchers—would argue that Bodoni is more readable because it is a serif face. The controversy over the comparative readability of serifs and sans serifs has been going on for years and can still raise hackles.

The pro-serif position has best been summarized by Ruari McLean, a notable British designer, in his *The Thames and Hudson Manual of Typography*:

> Sans-serif is intrinsically less legible [readable] than seriffed type. It is less legible because it is inherent in sans-serif type that some of the letters are more like each other than letters that have serifs, and so the certainty of decipherment is diminished. . . . We find that serifs have three prime functions: (1) they help to keep the letters a certain distance apart; (2) at the same time they link letters together to form words, which helps reading . . . and (3) they help to differentiate individual letters, particularly top halves, which is what we recognize words by. . . .

The argument at first blush seems fairly convincing, particularly when it is put forward by a designer of McLean's stature, but, like most of the arguments on this issue, it lacks objective support. I am not familiar with any studies that demonstrate the validity of (1) or (2); in fact, to claim both as readability factors seems a little like having your cake and eating it. It has been well-established that we read word-shapes, but only that we read the images as a whole, not the internal structures. It has also been shown that we recognize letter forms principally by the shape and dimensions of the counters; but counters are not the same thing as letterspacing. Point (3), on the other hand, has some validity, but may stretch the point too far. It is easy enough to demonstrate that you can reconstruct a word more easily from the top half than from the bottom half, as you can see for yourself:

gibberish   gibberish

ABSQUATULATE   ABSQUATULATE

But that is not quite the same thing as recognizing words exclusively by the top halves. And, in any case, the claim that serifs "help to differentiate individual letters" needs some scientific support.

Pro-sans-seriffers usually counter with a well-known study by Zachrisson in 1965 which demonstrated pretty convincingly that children prefer sans serifs. My feeling is that the study is significant in a different sense. Some fifty years ago, one of McLean's eminent predecessors, Eric Gill, wrote "Legibility [readability, again] may be a matter of nothing more than what one is accustomed to"; and that may be the heart of the matter. Far more text material is set in serif faces than in sans serifs. Most people learn to read from books set in serif faces. Consequently, their first inventory of word-shapes is essentially of seriffed forms (even though, oddly enough, most of them learned to write in what are essentially sans serif letters). However, sans serifs are being used more frequently for text, and, as they become more familiar, the whole controversy may simply shrivel up and blow away.

In the meantime, there seem to be no valid grounds for regarding any type family as inherently more readable than any other; far too many other factors have to be considered. On the other hand, it seems likely that most people, at least for the next few years, will find sans serif text slightly unusual, and that likelihood can be used to advantage.

In any typeface, however, the lower case is more readable than the upper case. Caps form word-shapes that are basically uniform rectangles, differentiated mainly by length. The lower

114

case, with its variegated array of single-component characters, ascenders, descenders and dotted letters, makes far more distinctive word-shapes.

a guide to type design

A GUIDE TO TYPE DESIGN

a guide to type design

A GUIDE TO TYPE DESIGN

The difference is critical in text. In display, it is not as vital, again, because in the larger sizes of type, we tend to be less able to assemble the characters into coherent word-shapes.

Regular roman fonts are more readable than any of the variants. Here, familiarity may be the deciding factor. However, the roman font is almost invariably designed first, and, in this sense, is the basic form of the face. In fact, frequently the variants are added by other designers.

Italics are the least readable variant. The diagonal stress tends to conflict with the strict horizontals of the lines, and the lighter weight of the letters offers a less distinct contrast with the white background.

Boldfaces are generally more readable than light faces, which, like italics, contrast less strongly with the background of the page. In multiweight faces, they also lack the distinctive shading of the heavier fonts. Condensed fonts are generally more readable than extended fonts, although the distortion of the familiar letter-forms reduces the readability of both. Apparently a horizontal extension of the counters is less tolerable than a horizontal compression.

Ultrabolds and all other ultras are the least readable styles.

Four fonts of Goudy Old Style vary greatly in readability. The regular roman at top is clearer than the roman boldface and both are more readable than their italic counterparts.

Boldfacing, however, improves the readability of the italic because it provides a stronger contrast with the white paper.

Until the Roman alphabet is superseded by some different means of conveying thought there is little likelihood of any strikingly original development in the making of either type or books. Perhaps the designer of the future will be devoting his talent to the decoration of phonograph records, or scrolls such as the ancient Egyptians and Greeks and Romans used.

Until the Roman alphabet is superseded by some different means of conveying thought there is little likelihood of any strikingly original development in the making of either type or books. Perhaps the designer of the future will be devoting his talent to the decoration of phonograph records, or scrolls such as the ancient Egyptians and Greeks and Romans used.

Until the Roman alphabet is superseded by some different means of conveying thought there is little likelihood of any strikingly original development in the making of either type or books. Perhaps the designer of the future will be devoting his talent to the decoration of phonograph records, or scrolls such as the ancient Egyptians and Greeks and Romans used.

Until the Roman alphabet is superseded by some different means of conveying thought there is little likelihood of any strikingly original development in the making of either type or books. Perhaps the designer of the future will be devoting his talent to the decoration of phonograph records, or scrolls such as the ancient Egyptians and Greeks and Romans used.

Spacing

The Swiss typographer Jan Tschichold opens the introduction of his *Meisterbuch der Schrift* with these words:

> Good lettering demands three things. (1) Good letters . . . (2) Good design in all details. This calls for well-balanced and sensitive letter-spacing, and word-spacing which takes the letter-spacing into account. . . .

Significantly, he gives spacing second place on the list.

To the designer, the blank areas are more important than the printed forms. And with good reason. We now know that counters are the vital factor in legibility and that the balance of spaces within and between characters effectively create the word-shape.

However, no study so far has produced a usable formula for

spacing, so we still have to rely on the designer's ultimate tool—the eye.

The designer of a typeface spends (or used to spend) as much time testing the way the characters fit together as designing the letter-forms themselves, so, in a reasonably well-designed face, it is safe to assume that the "natural" letterspacing built in by the designer is the optimal spacing for most situations. And that assumption is really the only firm foundation you have. Word-spacing is a variable that must be proportionate to the letter-spacing. Linespacing is another variable, as is marginal spacing.

Letterspacing may have to be adjusted, but only in displays, and then mainly to correct awkward letter-fits.

Spacing decisions were somewhat simpler in the era of metal type because of the physical restrictions imposed by the rigidity of metal characters. They could not be fitted together more tightly than normal unless the edges were planed down or chunks were sawed out so that they could be interlocked like pieces of a jigsaw. Both operations were expensive and, of course, the type could not be re-used, so they were rarely prac- tical for run-of-the-mill typesetting. In text, words were divided with 3-em spaces, or 4-em spaces if the copy had to be set tightly, and that was that. Linespacing could be increased with leads, but it could not be reduced except, again, by planing down the type and ruining it.

In contrast, most contemporary typesetters offer at least three alternatives to normal spacing as a matter of course: loose (½ unit more than normal), tight (½ unit less), and very tight (1 unit less). Digital typesetters can be programmed with a few keystrokes to letterspace in fractions of units, plus or minus, to any degree you like. Word- and line-spacing can also be speci- fied at will, plus or minus, in fractions of units or points.

This versatility opens up all kinds of opportunities for crea- tive spacing. An entire spectrum of new type colors can be achieved by subtle linespacing. The ability to kern and overlap characters is invaluable for designing logotypes, magazine name- plates and similar displays were distinctiveness rather than read- ability is the prime criterion. However, once you depart from the familiar type parameters, it becomes increasingly difficult to predict the results. A small change in letterspacing subtly alters the balance of spacing overall; the other parameters must be adjusted accordingly, and finding a satisfactory new balance takes time and a considerable amount of expertise. Few designers have the leisure and the experience to indulge in extensive experimentation.

Admittedly, the power and speed of the more-advanced digital systems make experimentation considerably easier—if you have access to a system and the time to play with it. It is equally true, however, that the programs are devised by engineers rather than typographers, often at the demand of marketing departments anxious to keep a competitive edge over rival manufacturers. The interests of the reader, I suspect, are not of paramount importance.

Advertising art directors, with their characteristic flair for innovation (and their weakness for novelty) have not been slow to

It has often been said that printing, as well as other arts, reflects the tastes and tendencies of its time. As life at present is more nervous, self-assertive, and generally disorganized than ever before, it is not strange that our printing should exhibit the same characteristics.

It has often been said that printing, as well as other arts, reflects the tastes and tendencies of its time. As life at present is more nervous, self-assertive, and generally disorganized than ever before, it is not strange that our printing should exhibit the same characteristics.

The first passage is set with traditional 6-unit wordspaces and normal letterspacing. The second is set to the same specifications but with automatic kerning; notice the tighter punctuation and the spacing of the ev in line 4. The third section is tight-spaced throughout and makes for less comfortable reading. The last is very tight-spaced; if the wordspacing were equally tight, we would have typographic gibberish.

It has often been said that printing, as well as other arts, reflects the tastes and tendencies of its time. As life at present is more nervous, self-assertive, and generally disorganized than ever before, it is not strange that our printing should exhibit the same characteristics.

It has often been said that printing, as well as other arts, reflects the tastes and tendencies of its time. As life at present is more nervous, self-assertive, and generally disorganized than ever before, it is not strange that our printing should exhibit the same characteristics.

experiment. Their influence, however, seems to have resulted in a general trend to tight spacing for tight spacing's sake; certainly, their demands have influenced both manufacturers and typesetters. But, with all due respect to my colleagues in that field, advertising is not the most vital form of print communication, and what is appropriate for promotional blurbs may not be suitable for other forms of reading matter.

In the first place, kerning distorts the inherent balance of internal and external spacing built into the design of the face. Logically, if you tamper with the normal spacing, you must adjust the counters reciprocally—in effect redesigning the face. That way lies typographic anarchy.

Perhaps worse, familiar word-shapes are subtly, but decisively, changed, and the reader is forced to learn a new vocabulary of word-shapes with every degree of kerning. At best, he or she has to pick a slower path through the type.

To compound the difficulty, when letters are tight-spaced, words must also be tight-spaced, sometimes to the point at which the divisions between the words are no wider than some of the spaces within the words. The line degenerates into a string of characters with no easily recognizable breaks between words. Here is the same text, normally letterspaced, with 6 unit, 4.5 unit, and 3.6 unit word spaces.

The best printing follows traditional lines because printing is a conservative as well as preservative art, and these lines are the result of innumerable efforts in the past to produce the best, conditioned by the materials at hand and the capabilities of the producer himself.

The best printing follows traditional lines because printing is a conservative as well as preservative art, and these lines are the result of innumerable efforts in the past to produce the best, conditioned by the materials at hand and the capabilities of the producer himself.

The best printing follows traditional lines because printing is a conservative as well as preservative art, and these lines are the result of innumerable efforts in the past to produce the best, conditioned by the materials at hand and the capabilities of the producer himself.

By all means, use minus-spacing if there is a sound reason for doing so. There is, after all, only one universal rule in type—if it works, it's right. But don't use it simply because it is available. Spacing is already complicated enough as it is.

There is really only one general rule of spacing: letter-, word-, and line-spacing must be balanced but well differentiated.

The basic unit must be the normal letterspacing of the face. Generally, you will not tamper with it, and then only in displays, and with discretion. The traditional standard for a rhythmically balanced word is that the main upright strokes should look uniformly spaced. Most typefaces are designed with this standard in mind.

Wordspacing must divide the words clearly. It must be clearly wider than any counter or letter space. It should also be uniform; even in justified type, where the word spaces have to be adjusted to fill the line, it should not be noticeably irregular.

Linespacing should never be identical with or close to the wordspacing. If the two are approximately equal, the reader's eye will drop through the wordspaces and into the linespace below.

These general principles apply to any style of typesetting, but in many other respects, text spacing is very different from display spacing so we will tackle them separately.

Text spacing   Normal letterspacing should be used for running text, even if it is brief. The only valid reason for adjusting it is to avoid the excessive wordspaces that often crop up in short lines of justified type. In conformity with Murphy's Law, large wordspaces tend to coincide on successive lines, opening up fissures in the type, called rivers. European typesetters routinely letterspace to cure this problem; American typesetters generally won't hear of it. Even so, I strongly recommend it.

Rivers not only destroy the texture of the type, they also drag the reader's eye down. If your typesetter won't letterspace offending lines, reset the text to get rid of the rivers one way or another and let the typesetter absorb the expense.

The conventional wordspace is a 3-em, or 6-unit, space, which works well with virtually any normally letterspaced text face. However, typesetters seem to be moving toward tighter wordspacing generally, even with unkerned type. The tightest

If the type page is to be quite narrow then the type may be a slightly condensed or a closely fitted one; but narrow or closely set type in a long line looks as though you might have been more generous. A formula might be deduced, that the rectangular proportions of your type should harmonize with the rectangular proportions of your type page—but beware of following formulas too literally.

If the type page is to be quite narrow then the type may be a slightly condensed or a closely fitted one; but narrow or closely set type in a long line looks as though you might have been more generous. A formula might be deduced, that the rectangular proportions of your type should harmonize with the rectangular proportions of your type page—but beware of following formulas too literally.

The left-hand column has a long river running through the center and smaller rivers in the last three lines. These have been eliminated in the right column simply by letterspacing the seventh, tenth, and seventeenth lines.

acceptable wordspace is a 4-em (4.5 unit) space, and there is no good reason to specify it unless you have miscalculated the copy-fit and can't think of any other solution.

Bold faces and the heavier sans serifs sometimes read more easily with slightly looser wordspacing (but no more than 6.5 units and never if the text is justified). If you decide on looser spacing, have the typesetter set a short sample and take a good look at it before committing yourself.

Linespacing offers no problems if the text is set solid. Normally, however, you will be adding some linespace to your type. A practical formula for linespacing has been suggested by Marshall Lee in his excellent *Bookmaking*:

☐ For 10- to 11-point type
add 1 point of linespacing on measures up to 22 picas
add 2 points of linespacing on measures of 22–25 picas
add 3 points of linespacing on measures over 25 picas

☐ For 12- to 14-point type
add 2 points of linespacing on measures up to 25 picas
add 3 points of linespacing on measures of 25–28 picas
add 4 points of linespacing on measures over 28 picas

The amount of leading that a page requires depends on so many factors that it is difficult to give any fixed method of procedure. The kind of type, the size of type, the length of line and the general character of the text all bear on this point.

Generally speaking, most types should be at least slightly leaded, especially if the lines are fairly long. This helps the eye to catch the following line in rapid reading more easily than when the type is set solidly.

The solid pages were usually adopted when old-style types were used exclusively; but when modern type came in, beginning with Bodoni, the custom of leading, sometimes double-leading, arose.

The amount of leading that a page requires depends on so many factors that it is difficult to give any fixed method of procedure. The kind of type, the size of type, the length of line and the general character of the text all bear on this point.

Generally speaking, most types should be at least slightly leaded, especially if the lines are fairly long. This helps the eye to catch the following line in rapid reading more easily than when the type is set solidly.

The solid pages were usually adopted when old-style types were used exclusively; but when modern type came in, beginning with Bodoni, the custom of leading, sometimes double-leading, arose. The effect of these new types was helped by a generous amount of white paper between the lines.

The Lee formulas, with Caslon as the typeface. The specifications from top to bottom are: 10/11 x 22 picas, 10/12 x 24 picas, 10/13 x 28 picas, 13/15 x 24 picas, 13/16 x 27 picas, and 13/17 x 32 picas. As the last three demonstrate, the formulas work equally well with nonstandard sizes.

This applies to Bodoni, Bulmer, and the Scotch face and their derivatives. Antique types were, however, occasionally very freely leaded, especially in Spanish books of the late fifteenth and early sixteenth centuries.

This applies to Bodoni, Bulmer, and the Scotch face and their derivatives. Antique types were, however, occasionally very freely leaded, especially in Spanish books of the late fifteenth and early sixteenth centuries.

The 8 point type set solid is almost indecipherable; the lower version, with 3 points of linespacing offers no problems. At the opposite extreme, the 10 point Caslon bold on a 24 pica line also benefits from 3 points of linespacing.

The amount of leading that a page requires depends on so many factors that it is difficult to give any fixed method of procedure. The kind of type, the size of type, the length of line and the general character of the text all bear on this point.

The amount of leading that a page requires depends on so many factors that it is difficult to give any fixed method of procedure. The kind of type, the size of type, the length of line and the general character of the text all bear on this point.

Smaller type sizes need proportionately more linespacing, especially on short measures.

Boldfaces also need more linespacing than their regular counterparts.

However, overgenerous linespacing makes reading difficult because it increases eye travel. Linespacing should never be more than the optical height of the type; that is, it should never look as though the line space were big enough to fit another line of type.

Generally speaking, most types should be at least slightly leaded, especially if the lines are fairly long. This helps the eye to catch the following line in rapid reading more easily than when the type is set solidly.

Generally speaking, most types should be at least slightly leaded, especially if the lines are fairly long. This helps the eye to catch the following line in rapid reading more easily than when the type is set solidly.

The Caslon at top is linespaced to formula. The lower version, with 7 points of linespacing, make it difficult to pick up the next line, though the measure is an "optimal" 24 picas.

Formula-linespaced Garamond looks too gray for comfort; the lower version, with only a half-point less (10/11½) is more evenly textured and readable.

This applies to Bodoni, Bulmer, and the Scotch face and their derivatives. Antique types were, however, occasionally very freely leaded, especially in Spanish books of the late fifteenth and early sixteenth centuries.

This applies to Bodoni, Bulmer, and the Scotch face and their derivatives. Antique types were, however, occasionally very freely leaded, especially in Spanish books of the late fifteenth and early sixteenth centuries.

Generally, you should linespace moderns, square serifs, and sans serifs as a matter of course. Some transitionals and most oldstyles are perfectly readable set solid, but few typefaces look worse if they are linespaced. Perhaps the only exceptions are the Venetian oldstyles with their long ascenders and descenders. Some of them look washed-out if they are widely linespaced; as a general rule, specify a quarter- or half-point less linespacing for the more venerable old styles.

Columns of justified type should be separated by about 1.5 picas if the measure is 13 picas or less; for longer measures, use about 1.5 picas, but never much more than that if the text reads continuously from one column to the next. When the type is set ragged right, the spacing can be reduced slightly because the indented right margin adds some space. If you run a rule between the columns, add at least another half-pica to the column spacing or the page will look crowded.

Margins are not really spaces in the same sense as letter-, word-, or line-spaces. These are aimed at producing a readable text; margins, on the other hand, are integral to the layout in general and the overall style of the design. There are, however, some general principles to keep in mind, and one formula.

Text pages are generally in a proportion of 2:3 (width:height) and the text occupies about half of the space. (It doesn't look that way, but if you find it hard to believe, measure up a few printed pages at random.) As the marginal area decreases, the page assumes a heavier look. Narrow margins are typical of text books, scholarly treatises, technical and reference works, and insurance guides. Multi-column formats reinforce the effect.

Interestingly, bibles, hymn books and other liturgical works, which used to have the stingiest of margins, are now appearing in more open designs, which may say something about shifting attitudes to matters religious. The general trend in any case is to a more generous use of white space (which may well say something equally significant about reading habits). There has been a similar trend to less regular margins and asymmetrical layouts.

As a general rule then, use smaller, balanced margins if you want a more serious look, and broader, unbalanced margins for a contemporary look.

If you want a purely conventional but eye-pleasing arrangement, you can't beat the Golden Section, which is a fairly simple formula rediscovered by Jan Tschichold after an intensive study of medieval manuscripts and early printed books. It has been used since time immemorial by calligraphers and typographers alike.

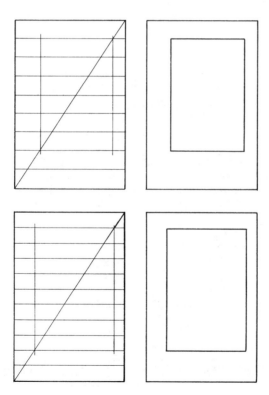

Two methods of constructing the Golden Section—the classic 9-division above, the less-common 11-division below.

First, divide the page into nine equal horizontal sections. (Seven and eleven sections also produces comparable results.) Then draw the diagonal from the top right corner, and run perpendiculars from the points where it intersects the top and next-to-bottom dividers. The resulting rectangle gives you a text-block almost exactly half the area of the page, and margins in a proportion of roughly 2 (inside): 3 (top): 4 (outside): 5 (bottom). In a conventional, centered two-page spread, the two gutter margins are equal to either outside margin, giving a pleasantly balanced appearance.

Simple, neat, and satisfactory.

Unfortunately, it is the only formula I know of, and, for any other arrangement, you will simply have to rely on your eye.

Display spacing In contrast to text, displays are often custom-spaced.

All-cap lines almost invariably need to be letterspaced for two reasons. First, spreading out the characters tends to make the word-shape slightly more distinctive and therefore more readable. Second, caps are prone to awkward letter fits. L's combined with virtually any other letter produce a gap in the word, and an LA combination will break a word's back. Any other cap with a large counter on either side (e.g., T, F) or sloping stems (e.g., A, K, W) will be a troublemaker. Curved characters can also cause problems.

At the other end of the scale, I's combined with other vertical strokes begin to form indecipherable thickets of stems.

Digital programs often kern some letter-pairs automatically, but this is a band-aid solution, as we will see later. Adding some space between characters alleviates the problem, but is merely a partial cure. The only real remedy is to adjust the spacing of each pair of characters individually. Tschichold calls the process "neutralizing"—respacing until there is no obvious irregularity (and he was a master of it)—but it is more generally known as optical spacing.

Some classic bad letterfits. Most digital typesetters automatically kern them—not always ideally—as in the second row.

LA	TW	AS	RT	ILL	IMMI
LA	TW	AS	RT	ILL	IMMI

The first step is to isolate the worse letter-fit. Here is an example:

ATLANTIC

Obviously the major offender is the classic bugbear, LA. However, the AT also needs looking at.

Automatic kerning would give us this:

ATLANTIC

That takes care of the AT but opens up another pair of gaps around the second T and has not fixed the LA. If anything, closing up the other letters exaggerates the gap by contrast. We should respace optically by closing up the LA as tightly as possible and using the corrected space as the basis for spacing all the other pairs. In other words, we now spread them until the spacing matches the adjusted LA spacing as closely as possible, like this:

ATLANTIC

Digital systems make optical spacing almost childishly easy, because you can work over the word in microseconds and print out the result quickly for a visual check. Sadly, very few people seem to be using them in this way. If you don't have access to a system, and you are not sure you can specify the correct spacing parameters by eye, resort to the tracing-paper technique. Lay a sheet of tracing paper over the offending word and trace down the worst letter-fit, moving the sheet left or right to close up the characters. When you are satisfied with the spacing, match up the pairs on either side in the same way, shifting the sheet until the last traced character is properly spaced with the printed character below, and then tracing that onto the sheet. It will usually take several tries, but you end up with a very precise layout to send to the typesetter, and you don't even have to specify the spacing.

Lower-case displays generally pose fewer letterspacing problems. Unlike cap displays, they should usually be letterspaced normally. Poor letterfits can be corrected by optical spacing.

Wordspacing is not automatic in displays; the uniform 3-em space is too rigid and perhaps too open. In any case, you may have tinkered with the letterspacing and will automatically have to adjust the wordspacing to balance.

Some designers use the width of the crossbar of the H as a wordspace in all-cap displays. As a quick-and-dirty guide, this works adequately, but it still makes for an uncomfortably rigid standard. A better system is to leave a space large enough to take an optically spaced I (for all-cap) or i (for lower-case lines). This method gives you a wordspace that is always proportionate to the letterspacing, even if you have tinkered with it.

BRUCEIROGERS
BRUCE ROGERS

designeriextraordinary
designer extraordinary

The I/i system calls for delicate judgement. If you don't trust your judgement, trace an I/i from the font you are working with and use it as a mechanical guide. After some practice, you should be able to dispense with the mechanical aid and "eye-ball" your wordspacing fairly accurately.

Boldfaces (particularly in the larger sizes) and extended faces need slightly more wordspacing than regular fonts. It is usually a good idea to add one or two units to the normal space.

Condensed faces are the sole exception to the wordspacing principle for displays. Use normal letter- and word-spacing throughout, even for all-cap displays. If you have the room for more generous spacing, the chances are that you shouldn't be using a condensed face in the first place.

Displays need more generous linespacing than text, unless you are looking for a crowded or monolithic effect. The Lee formula, scaled up proportionately, should be used as the minimal linespacing. Centered displays, particularly, should be given plenty of breathing room. In fact, as far as displays are concerned, you can forget about the "don't-linespace-deeper-than-the-size-of-the-type" principle altogether.

Text heads are a special case. They must be spaced to separate them visually from the preceding text and tie them to the following text. The space above and below should be distributed in a ratio somewhere between 3:2 and 5:2. Generally, the larger and bolder the head, the less space it needs around it. Less obtrusive heads need more space to give them prominence.

If the heads are set in position (in the text, or "in galleys"), the break in the text must be equivalent to a whole number of text lines. In other words, the point size of the head type plus the space above plus the space below must be a multiple of the depth of the text line. If not, the text following the head will not align with the text in the next column.

For example, if your text is set solid in 10-point type, every line is 10 points deep. Your heads are set in 14-point type. If you specified the spacing as 8 points above and 3 points below, the break for the head would be 25 points deep altogether (14 + 8 + 3). But 25 points is 2.5 lines of text. In other words, the text following the head would be half a line lower than it would normally be and half a line out of alignment with the text in the neighboring column (unless you had another head in that column).

The problem doesn't arise of course if you set the heads separately (as patches) and combine them with the text in the mechanical. Then you can align the text and juggle the heads optically into the breaks you have left.

The same precaution must be taken with any display material incorporated into the text, such as lists or long quotations. These are often set in a smaller size of type or a different font altogether. You can simplify your life by making the linespacing consistent with the text linespacing (so the depth of the lines is the same even if the size of the type is different) and allowing a line space or a half-line space above and below the displayed section.

Measure There are all sorts of formulas for the ideal line length. Magazine editors like: make the measure (in picas) twice the type size (in points). It's crude and mechanical, but it works surprisingly well. A more general formula is: make the measure 1½–2½ alphabets long. This formula, unlike the first, takes the set of the face into account.

There are a number of reasons why this formula works.

First, we can keep an area about 4″ wide in sharp focus without having to turn our heads. In other words, we can read a line about 24 picas long and find the start of the next line simply by moving our eyes back; in fact, the beginning of the next line has never really dropped out of focus.

Most common text faces run to about 60 characters on a 24 pica line, or less than our 2½ alphabet limit. Here are some of them:

	10 point	11 point	12 point
Garamond	68	62	56
Baskerville	67	61	56
Bodoni	70	63	58
Stymie	62	57	53
Univers 55	65	59	54

We also blink about 25 times a minute, or roughly once every 2.4 seconds. Every time we blink, of course, we lose sight of the text and we also have to refocus. In other words, a blink is a fairly serious interruption in the reading. However, a fluent

It is a truism that almost every face of type has its ideal size, and lessens in merit as this size is either increased or decreased. The modern practice of cutting all sizes (at least down to 8-point) from one pattern on a pantograph machine, is accountable for much of the mechanical appearance of our books. But before the pantograph was invented, each size, although based on one model, was really a separate design.

It is a truism that almost every face of type has its ideal size, and lessens in merit as this size is either increased or decreased. The modern practice of cutting all sizes (at least down to 8-point) from one pattern on a pantograph machine, is accountable for much of the mechanical appearance of our books. But before the pantograph was invented, each size, although based on one model, was really a separate design.

It is a truism that almost every face of type has its ideal size, and lessens in merit as this size is either increased or decreased. The modern practice of cutting all sizes (at least down to 8-point) from one pattern on a pantograph machine, is accountable for much of the mechanical appearance of our books. But before the pantograph was invented, each size, although based on one model, was really a separate design.

Small, tight-fitting faces like Bodoni read more comfortably on a shorter measure (center), while large faces like Melior (bottom) can be set on a "maximum" line.

reader reads about 10 words (which amount on the average to 60 characters) in 2.4 seconds. Fluent readers, then, can do their blinking while they are traveling back to the beginning of the next line.

Of course, there isn't any such thing as an ideal line length in the absolute sense. The best measure for 10 point Janson will probably not be the ideal line for 12 point Bulmer. However, if you keep your text measures between 20 picas and 26 picas, you won't go too far wrong.

Generally, you will use the shorter measures with smaller x-height faces, smaller point sizes and tight-setting fonts because you will usually reach the 2½ alphabet limit sooner. Larger faces—in any respect—need longer measures.

10 point Univers is perfectly readable on an optimal 24 pica line, but the readability improves on a slightly shorter (22 pica) line.

It is a truism that almost every face of type has its ideal size, and lessens in merit as this size is either increased or decreased. The modern practice of cutting all sizes (at least down to 8-point) from one pattern on a pantograph machine, is accountable for much of the mechanical appearance of our books. But before the pantograph was invented, each size, although based on one model, was really a separate design.

It is a truism that almost every face of type has its ideal size, and lessens in merit as this size is either increased or decreased. The modern practice of cutting all sizes (at least down to 8-point) from one pattern on a pantograph machine, is accountable for much of the mechanical appearance of our books. But before the pantograph was invented, each size, although based on one model, was really a separate design.

Italics, light faces and bold faces should be set on shorter measures than their roman equivalents to compensate for their lower readability. Monoweight sans serifs are also more comfortable to read on shorter measures.

Ragged-right text should be set shorter than its justified equivalent so that the reader never loses the left margin. Other unjustified settings—if you are foolhardy enough to use them for text—should be set on measures no longer than 75 percent of the justified equivalent.

In multicolumn formats, you probably won't have room for 20–25 pica measures, but your column should never be less than 11 picas; that is, somewhat more than half the optimal measure.

When lines are shorter than 11 picas, the reader's eye-movement increases sharply, which is fatiguing. Reading flow is constantly interrupted by line breaks, and the number of end-of-line hyphenations increases, slowing the reader even more. If, for some unfathomable reason, you insist on using a very short line, at least specify a tight-setting face and set the type ragged right to keep the wordspacing uniform. Preferably, select a face, such as Times Roman, which was designed for newspaper work where narrow columns are the norm.

If the type page is to be quite narrow then the type may be a slightly condensed or a closely fitted one; but narrow or closely set type in a long line looks as though you might have been more generous. A formula might be deduced, that the rectangular proportions of your type should harmonize with the rectangular proportions of your type page—but beware of following formulas too literally.

If the type page is to be quite narrow then the type may be a slightly condensed or a closely fitted one; but narrow or closely set type in a long line looks as though you might have been more generous. A formula might be deduced, that the rectangular proportions of your type should harmonize with the rectangular proportions of your type page—but beware of following formulas too literally.

Excessively long lines make life equally difficult for the reader. In the first place, if the line is much longer than 26 picas, the left margin is out of focus. The reader must move his or her head to bring the beginning of the next line into view and, as likely as not, will pick up the wrong line. By the time the realization sinks in, he or she has forgotten what the first line said and has to go back to read it again, starting the whole frustrating cycle over again. If, for some equally unfathomable reason, you must have a long measure, use a larger-than-normal type and plenty of linespacing so that the lines are well separated.

Displays should follow the same basic principle: the line should be within the sharp focus of the eye. Obviously, it won't usually be 1½–2½ alphabets long. The measure is dictated by the reading distance and can be calculated fairly simply.

Text heads—again—are a special case. Heads should never be as long as the accompanying text measure; otherwise they do not stand out from the mass of text.

If the type page is to be quite narrow then the type may be a slightly condensed or a close-ly fitted one; but narrow or closely set type in a long line looks as though you might have been more generous. A formula might be deduced, that the rectangular proportions of your type should harmonize with the rectangular proportions of your type page—but beware of following formulas too literally.

If the type page is to be quite narrow then the type may be a slightly condensed or a close-ly fitted one; but narrow or closely set type in a long line looks as though you might have been more generous. A formula might be deduced, that the rectangular proportions of your type should harmonize with the rectangular proportions of your type page—but beware of following formulas too literally.

Inordinately long lines must be generously linespaced to be readable.

If a head runs to more than two-thirds of the text measure, it should be turned; the run-on line should always be shorter than the first line. As far as possible, however, the break should be determined by the sense of the words. Coherent phrases, such as adjective/noun combinations, should not be divided. Always try to start the run-on with a major word (i.e., something other than a short preposition or a particle), an article (the, a, an) or a conjunction.

If a head runs to more than two lines, shoot the writer or editor.

Setting There are essentially five formats for type:

☐ justified
☐ flush left, ragged right
☐ flush right, ragged left
☐ centered
☐ free form

Only the first two can be considered readable formats for text because they have a fixed left margin as a constant reference point for the beginning of new lines.

Justified text has been the norm since Gutenberg, and actually since long before him. Virtually all manuscripts were written in justified formats; much of the decoration simply served to fill out lines. Justified pages, then, are by far the most familiar, and therefore the most transparent, from the standpoint of the reader. There is something endlessly satisfying about the neatly ordered rectangles of type with their consistent margins. And, from a purely pragmatic point of view, justified type is easier to copyfit because all the lines are the same length. Moreover, it blends naturally with square halftones and artwork, the most common forms of illustration.

Justification's major drawback is the inevitable irregularity of the wordspacing. Few lines fit the measure precisely with regular wordspacing, and they have to be squeezed or stretched by adding to or subtracting from the wordspaces. The alternative is to break and hyphenate words at the end of lines. As a result, reading is made a little more difficult—although most readers are not consciously bothered—and the texture of the type block is marred.

Hyphenation and justification (H&J) is generally handled by a computer in contemporary typesetting systems, sometimes with peculiar results. There are basically two levels of programming; logic programs and exception dictionaries. Logic programs simply give the computer basic rules for breaking and hyphenating words, but language often defies logic. For example, words are generally hyphenated after the prefix en-, but a logic program can't distinguish between 'endear' and 'ending' and will hyphenate both after the en-. Exception dictionaries, which are more expensive, provide the computer with a vocabulary of words that are not broken according to the logic rules. Even these, however, can't deal with the innumerable oddities that can result from correct, but mindless, hyphenation. James Craig, in his *Production for the Graphic Designer*, cites a classic example—therapist—which, if hyphenated unwisely, produces the potentially libelous "the- rapist", and there are hundreds of other similar gaffes (beat-itude, can-died, sex-tant and so on). H&J programs also have a nasty habit of breaking numbers unintelligibly, leaving "$1-" at the end of one line and "billion" on the next. Perhaps the silliest error is something like this, which appeared recently in my local paper:[*]

"But," Mr. Blank added, "We have to ask 'Who profits
?'."

---

[*] Presumably the typesetter's program allowed an end-of-paragraph line if it was at least four characters long.

The remedy is to make sure your typesetter has a comprehensive H&J program beforehand and check your proofs meticulously.

Ragged-right settings are not prone to these problems. However, they are not as familiar to most readers in running text, although there is nothing particularly novel about the format. The first magazine set ragged right appeared almost a hundred years ago, and the first major book—appropriately enough, Eric Gill's *Essay On Typography*—over half a century ago. In fact, certain types of text, such as poetry and play scripts, have traditionally been set ragged right, and virtually all typewritten copy is too.

Ragged-right settings are more dynamic than justified text because of the contrast between the aligned left margin and the sawtooth right edge. The type is also more smoothly textured because the wordspacing is uniform and there is little or no end-of-line hyphenation.

The major drawback is that the right margin can become a tattered-right margin in the hands of an inexperienced or insensitive typesetter. You can anticipate the possibility to some extent by specifying a maximum and minimum limit to the measure, but in that case you will have to accept some end-of-line hyphenation.

Ideally, the right margin should form a gentle concave curve from top to bottom. You can achieve it by copyfitting carefully and marking the line breaks yourself, but this solution is only practical if the text is fairly short. With a long text, you simply cross your fingers and hope.

Some readers may be bothered by the irregular eye travel from the end of the lines, but the discomfort can be minimized by specifying a maximum/minimum line.

From a purely practical point of view, the major difficulty you will run across is copyfitting. You can't forecast precisely where the typesetter will break the lines, unless you are prepared to copyfit and mark the whole text line-for-line, so your copyfitting calculations can be way off in a lengthy text. To allow for the variable, I deduct three characters for every line of text, and, so far, this admittedly rough-and-ready system has not let me down.

Ideally, the right margin should form a gentle concave curve from top to bottom. You can achieve it by copyfitting carefully and marking the line breaks yourself, but this solution is only practical if the text is fairly short.

Ideally, the right margin should form a gentle concave curve from top to bottom. You can achieve it by copyfitting carefully and marking the line breaks yourself, but this solution is only practical if the text is fairly short.

Both of these displays are set to the same basic specifications, but the lower version was copy-fitted and marked for line breaks accordingly. The word-spacing of most lines was also adjusted to achieve the smooth curve, and final touches added by cutting-and-pasting the mechanical.

Which setting should you choose? Again, that depends.

In broad terms, if you need an unobtrusive, conventional, conservative, or serious-looking page, you should justify the text. If you want something more dynamic, more informal, or more contemporary in style, set it ragged right.

However, the general layout of the page will heavily influence its appearance. Justified text in an asymmetrical layout with broad margins will be anything but sober, while a ragged-right text in a balanced multi-column format can be very businesslike.

Typeface, setting and format can be played off each other in endless combinations to produce a wide spectrum of effects.

Justified and ragged-right settings can also be used for display, and with much the same effects.

Centered settings are the most formal of all displays. Title pages, formal invitations, official notices and professional business cards and letterheads were at one time invariably centered; many still are. (So too were tombstones, at one end of the scale, and playbills and theater posters, at the other, presumably in a bid for respectability, posthumous or otherwise.)

Centering inevitably creates a feeling of gravity or a sense of period. It requires a delicate touch in the balance of typefaces and sizes, and even more so in the vertical spacing of the lines. A well-executed centered display is perhaps the most elegant of

THE

HOLY BIBLE

Containing the Old and New Testaments: Translated out of the Original Tongues and with the former Translations diligently compared and revised by His Majesty's special Command

Appointed to be read in Churches

This dignified centered display is from the title page of the Oxford University Press's Lectern Bible. It was designed by Bruce Rogers whose comments on type design have been used for the type samples in this book. The typeface is a modified version of his Centaur.

designs, and the best designers have all been expert at it. (There are some superb examples in Stanley Morison's *Four Centuries of Fine Printing*, and, in a more modern vein, in Tschichold's *Treasury of Alphabets and Lettering*.) Poorly executed centered displays, on the other hand, are the dullest form of design.

Ragged-left settings are rarely dull. They are perhaps the most unconventional of settings, because they violate the ingrained pattern of reading. They are often used to balance ragged-right settings on the opposite side of a spread or layout. For example, in balanced spreads with wide outside margins, the heads are often hung in the margin, ragged right and ragged left on the facing pages as they are in this book. Captions butted up to the left side of illustrations are often set ragged left.

Generally, however, keep ragged-left settings for those occasions when you really want to catch the reader's eye. And break the lines according to the principles for two-line heads discussed earlier.

Free-form displays are the least readable of all settings because they have no uniform reference points at the beginning or the end of the lines. They should be used only where impact is far more important than readability; short runs of advertising copy, captions in photo essays, blurbs on record covers or posters, and call-outs in magazine stories.

They are extremely difficult to integrate into a layout because they offer no consistent points of alignment, particularly vertical alignment. You can use the first character of the line protruding farthest to the left or the last character of the line protruding farthest to the right, but these are tenuous alignments at best. The optical axis of the type (that is, the imaginary vertical line that divides the type block into two equal masses) is another possible alignment point. You can locate it roughly by laying a sheet of tracing paper over the type block and moving it slowly to the left until the covered type seems to balance the uncovered type. Ultimately, however, a free-form type block has to be positioned by eye.

Two fairly common subspecies of free-form setting are contoured settings and runarounds. A contoured setting is arranged in the shape of a recognizable object. A classic example is the mouse's "long and sad tale" in *Alice's Adventures in Wonderland*.

The contoured cup was a classic challenge for hand typesetters. This version was produced with considerably less effort on a computerized page-makeup system, Compugraphic's AdVantage.

Don't try to 'design' every page of type throughout
a book or work it over too carefully after the style
is chosen; leave something to accident, so long as
it is not a glaring defect. The proof-reader and
the workman in the shop, if they have been properly instructed, usually may be trusted to
take care of the ordinary details of arrangement. You must, however, guard against
the tendency to bring out all the final
lines of a paragraph or a page to full
measure, for many printers want
everything squared up and tidy.
This is the emergence, again of
the mechanical faculty, and
some proof-readers have
been known to go
over every page
with a
magni-
f y i n g
g l a s s
to be
s u r e
there is
not the
l e a s t
imperf-
ection
in any of the letters.
This is the acme of fastidiousness
and is carrying perfection too far.

Contouring demands extremely precise copyfitting, and, even with digital typesetters, is time-consuming and expensive. It usually doesn't warrant the time or expense.

Free-form runarounds are relatively common in magazines and glossy brochures where irregularly shaped artwork pro-trudes into the text. The effect is artificial and, again, rarely jus-tifies the effort involved. It draws immediate attention, but the irregular lines are extremely difficult to read.

Heads are generally set centered, ragged right (or, more cor-rectly, flush left), and occasionally ragged left (flush right). Cen-tered heads, like all centered settings, are the most formal. They should be combined only with justified text; with ragged-right settings, they always look slightly off-center. Turned lines are usually centered under the first line, except in newspapers, where they are sometimes justified—and known, appropriately enough, as tombstones.

Flush-left heads are compatible with any text setting. They are particularly effective in a face that contrasts sharply with the text face. (Centered heads are often set in the same face as the text, or a closely allied face.) Turned lines are usually set flush left, although they may also be indented slightly for a decorative

Centered Heads

Centered heads, like all centered settings, are the most formal. They should be combined only with justified text; with ragged-right settings, they always look slightly off-center. Turned lines are usually centered under the first line, except in newspapers, where they are sometimes justified—and known, appropriately enough, as tombstones.

CENTERED HEADS

Centered heads, like all centered settings, are the most formal. They should be combined only with justified text; with ragged-right settings, they always look slightly.off-center. Turned lines are usually centered under the first line, except in newspapers, where they are sometimes justified—and known, appropriately enough, as tombstones.

Centered Heads

Centered heads, like all centered settings, are the most formal. They should be combined only with justified text; with ragged-right settings, they always look slightly off-center. Turned lines are usually centered under the first line, except in newspapers, where they are sometimes justified—and known, appropriately enough, as tombstones.

Centered Heads

Centered heads, like all centered settings, are the most formal. They should be combined only with justified text; with ragged-right settings, they always look slightly off-center. Turned lines are usually centered under the first line, except in newspapers, where they are sometimes justified—and known, appropriately enough, as tombstones.

At top, the classic, formal, centered head. Larger heads (top center) or contrasting typefaces tend to soften the formality. Centered heads look off balance with unjustified text (bottom center) and the effect is exaggerated with a bolder or contrasting face; in this case, the choice of Baskerville bold is particularly unfortunate because transitionals generally do not blend happily with oldstyles.

effect. However, with justified text, they should be set consistently flush left.

Heads hung completely in the margin should be set flush left and aligned at the top with the cap line of the first line of text. In a symmetrical spread, the heads on the right-hand pages should be set flush right to maintain the balance of the layout. However, there is a problem; until the text is paged, you don't know which heads fall on the right-hand pages. If the schedule

Flush-left heads are generally less formal, even when set in the same typeface as the text (top center). Sharp contrasts in typeface, size or weight are even less formal and open up the design. Extreme contrasts should be avoided, however, because the heads will overwhelm the text, particularly if the text passages are short. One remedy is to set oversized heads in a tint or color (bottom).

FLUSH-LEFT HEADS

Flush-left heads are compatible with any text setting. They are particularly effective in a face that contrasts sharply with the text face. (Centered heads are often set in the same face as the text, or a closely allied face.) Turned lines are usually set flush left, although they may also be indented slightly for a decorative effect. However, with justified text, they should be set consistently flush left.

FLUSH-LEFT HEADS

Flush-left heads are compatible with any text setting. They are particularly effective in a face that contrasts sharply with the text face. (Centered heads are often set in the same face as the text, or a closely allied face.) Turned lines are usually set flush left, although they may also be indented slightly for a decorative effect. However, with justified text, they should be set consistently flush left.

Flush-Left Heads

Flush-left heads are compatible with any text setting. They are particularly effective in a face that contrasts sharply with the text face. (Centered heads are often set in the same face as the text, or a closely allied face.) Turned lines are usually set flush left, although they may also be indented slightly for a decorative effect. However, with justified text, they should be set consistently flush left.

FLUSH-LEFT HEADS

Flush-left heads are compatible with any text setting. They are particularly effective in a face that contrasts sharply with the text face. (Centered heads are often set in the same face as the text, or a closely allied face.) Turned lines are usually set flush left, although they may also be indented slightly for a decorative effect. However, with justified text, they should be set consistently flush left.

allows, don't set any heads until paging is complete. Otherwise, all the right-hand heads will have to be reset.

Minor heads can be run into the text. You can differentiate them from the text in a number of ways—by boldfacing or underscoring, or setting in caps or small caps. You can also set bullets, quads or even dingbats in front if you want them to stand out.

As a general rule, it is better to set them in the same face and point size as the text to avoid linespacing problems, unless, of course, the section is separated from the preceding text by a line space. Even then, a larger type tends to look awkward. And, if you choose a different face, make sure that it aligns on the baseline of the text.

The difference between cooking and haute cuisine is often nothing more than a touch of spice. Similarly, in type, the difference between good design and ordinary design is a handful of small refinements. Here are some of them.

Finishing Touches

Hyphens, dashes, parentheses, brackets and braces are aligned with the lower case. When they are combined with all-cap lines, they look out of position. You can ask the typesetter to reposition them, which is simple to do on a digital system. If your typesetter is not digital, it is probably simpler and less expensive to fix them by cutting-and-pasting in the mechanical.

LETTER-SPACING OFTEN MISUSED

LETTER-SPACING OFTEN MISUSED

The hyphen in the lower line has been moved up to align with the crossbar of the Es to correct the off-center appearance of the first line.

Bullets, boxes and quads must be specified to align with the following type line—on the x-height in lower case and on the crossbar of the H in caps. Boxes to be filled in or checked off by the reader should align with the ascender/descender lines in lower-case copy and with the cap line and base line in all-cap settings.

In justified blocks of display copy, the smaller punctuation points (periods, commas, quotes, apostrophes, hyphens and asterisks) create untidy gaps at the beginnings and ends of lines. Moving them into the margin gives you an optically flush edge to the type.

The punctuation in the right-hand display has been hung slightly in the margins to produce optically flush edges to the type.

"In justified blocks of display copy, the smaller punctuation points (periods, commas, quotes, apostrophes, hyphens and asterisks) create untidy gaps at the beginnings and ends of lines. Moving them into the margin gives you an optically flush edge to the type."

"In justified blocks of display copy, the smaller punctuation points (periods, commas, quotes, apostrophes, hyphens and asterisks) create untidy gaps at the beginnings and ends of lines. Moving them into the margin gives you an optically flush edge to the type."

Slanted or curved characters at the beginning of lines in stacked displays also seem to be misaligned. They should be edged into the margin slightly; you will have to use your own judgment how far to move them.

The counters of the Ts and G give the type an optically concave left margin, even though the type is actually aligned. At right, the three middle lines have been shifted out to align optically.

A
GUIDE
TO
TYPE
DESIGN

A
GUIDE
TO
TYPE
DESIGN

If it works, it's right.
If it works, it's right.

In large displays, particularly in boldface type, the normal punctuation points tend to look oversized. Reduce the punctuation by one point size if you are working with 24-point or larger type or any heavy boldface. You will have to allow for the difference in unit size between the punctuation and the rest of the type, but again the problem can be solved by cut-and-paste.

The second line has been supplied with punctuation two sizes smaller than the letters for an optically consistent effect.

Italics are the conventional style for emphasis, but in a mass of type they simply disappear. Try boldfacing or even small caps for emphasis.

The start of a new paragraph is usually signalled with a 1-em indent. However, there are several other methods of paragraphing, if you are looking for something slightly out of the ordinary. You can use a deeper indent, although it should not be more than 5 ems. (A five-character indent is fairly common in typewritten copy.) A potential danger is the large gap produced by a short end-of-paragraph line, like the one above. In Europe, it is customary to set paragraphs flush out and separated by a line space. The effect is slightly severe. And don't use it if you have in-text heads. ¶For a decorative, if slightly eccentric effect, set the text continuously, separating paragraphs with paragraph marks or dingbats (but only if the copy is short.¶In long stretches of copy, however, this technique soon wears the reader down.)

An oversize initial is a striking and elegant way to begin a major section of text. It can be raised, that is, sticking up above the text; dropped, or set into the text; or hung in the margin.

A raised initial stands on the baseline of the first line of text, although it does not have to be in the same face; in fact, the decorative effect is greater if it is in a contrasting face. It should be at least twice the point size of the text, but it should not be too large or there will be an oversized gap between the following text and the preceding section. Generally, raised initials work best at the very beginning of a major section, with no text above.

A DROPPED INITIAL, depending on its size, aligns with the ascenders of the first line of text and the baseline of the second, third, fourth or fifth line. (It should rarely be taller than five lines or it will be completely out of proportion.) For some reason, dropped initials tend to look better if they are an odd number of lines deep. Slanted or open-sided caps need to be cheated out slightly into the margin or they will look misaligned; the following text characters can be kerned up to them to avoid an unsightly gap on the right. Digital typesetters can usually kern automatically to butt the shorter lines up to the initial. Otherwise, you will have to copyfit these lines very carefully and mark the breaks for the typesetter. It is often faster and simpler to specify the space for the initial and paste it into the mechanical.

It is probably wiser to set dropped initials in the same face as the text, since they read directly into the rest of the word. By tradition, the word or words following a dropped initial are often set in caps or small caps for coherence.

H ANGING INITIALS obviously need a wide outside margin. They align at the top with the ascenders of the first line of text; however, if the first word is in caps, they align with the cap line. (Don't use small caps or the initial will look misaligned with the text.) Avoid hanging initials if a high percentage have slanted stems (hanging A's, V's and W's simply float away from the text) or introduce short words (that is, fewer than four characters).

If your dropped or raised initial is the indefinite article "a", make sure it is clearly separated from the first word of text by

A GUIDE TO TYPE DESIGN

A GUIDE TO TYPE DESIGN

A GUIDE TO TYPE DESIGN

A GUIDE TO TYPE DESIGN

In slanted or vertical displays, the characters should be oriented normally. Bolder faces tend to be more readable than light faces.

adding a hairline space. You won't have any separation problem if it is hung.

And never use a numeral as an oversized initial numeral if it is part of a longer number.

The letters of the roman alphabet were designed to be read from left to right on the same baseline. Never set them vertically or on a slant. If you want a vertical or diagonal line, set the type in its normal orientation and then move the line as a whole into position.

Reversed type is, according to a recent study, 40 percent less readable than black type on a white background, although I am not entirely certain what "40 percent less" means. However, we do know that white figures on a black background 'shrink' optically. They may in fact be physically reduced because dense areas of ink tend to creep and invade the edges of the characters. If you specify reversed type, make it at least one point size larger than normal to offset the shrinking effect. If you are

Increasing the size of reversed type improves readability—but there is rarely a sound reason for reversing type anyway.

The text pages of most books should be printed in black ink. The tendency of a young printer is often to try for novelty by printing with color rather than with black, not realizing that most types were not designed for anything but black on white.

The text pages of most books should be printed in black ink. The tendency of a young printer is often to try for novelty by printing with color rather than with black, not realizing that most types were not designed for anything but black on white.

printing on an absorbent paper or an antique stock, move up still another size because the ink is more likely to spread.

The same principle applies if you print in a colored ink or on a colored paper; the type must be larger since the contrast is weaker.

The use of color introduces a host of problems, physical and psychological. Many colors appear to sink into the page while others float above it, and the effect is particularly noticeable if the type is reversed on a block of color or printed in a second color and mixed with black type. Colors also have strong emotional connotations. Some are cultural—red for danger, yellow for cowardice—but some appear to be physiological. Women seem to respond positively to certain colors, men to others. (There may be a physiological difference in the responses, as there is to sound; women can detect high-pitched sounds beyond the range of the normal male's capability.) Age is another factor; children like flat, bright, straightforward shades while their parents prefer more subtle colors.

The text pages of most books should be printed in black ink. The tendency of a young printer is often to try for novelty by printing with color rather than with black, not realizing that most types were not designed for anything but black on white.

Reversed type on tints or colors is even less readable because of the lack of contrast. In the lower, more readable version, the type has been set two sizes larger and could probably have been larger still.

The text pages of most books should be printed in black ink. The tendency of a young printer is often to try for novelty by printing with color rather than with black, not realizing that most types were not designed for anything but black on white.

The moral is: avoid color unless there is some overwhelming functional reason for using it and be very careful that the colors you choose will not have an unforeseen effect on the reader.

Few designs can be executed in a single font of type, but few need more than two faces (unless you are parodying a colonial playbill or a Victorian advertisement).

It is extraordinarily difficult to find three typefaces that work together harmoniously; the chances are that three or more typefaces will produce a visual hodgepodge. There are enough variations of size, weight, and style in any typeface to give you all the variety you could want, and more than enough in two typefaces.

Short lines (usually end-of-paragraph lines) at the top of a page or column—known chauvinistically as "widows"—are unsightly. The simplest way to deal with them is to move them back to the end of the preceding column or page. However, remember that you must add a line to every other type block on the spread to make them all even in depth. As long as all the columns on the same spread are consistent, the reader will never realize that they are slightly longer or shorter.

Nobody has ever defined the length of a widow precisely. Some designers—particularly in book publishing—consider anything less than a full line to be a widow. Magazine and newspaper designers will often leave anything more than two-thirds of the measure. When the text is justified, I leave a widow alone if it is not more than five characters short of the measure; in a ragged-right setting, I will accept a widow more than about four-fifths of the maximum measure. However, if the measures are short (less than 13 picas), I generally move back any line short of the full measure.

COMMUNICATING THE DESIGN

After much soul-searching, head-scratching and struggle, you have a design. But the work is far from finished. Unless you plan to set the type yourself—and that option may become commonplace in the near future—you have to communicate your ideas to someone else.* In type language, you have to "mark copy".

Over the centuries, a fairly standardized system of copymarking has been established. It is based, like much else in typography, on metal typesetting. Digital typesetting, however, has introduced an entirely novel approach to the subject. Happily (or unhappily, depending on how much of a pessimist you are), almost every digital system has its own particular set of symbols and terms. Relatively few are standard; flush left, flush right, and centered have become quad left, quad right, and quad center, but apart from that the terminology tends to be specific to the system.

As a result, we are still using the traditional system for the most part. It is fairly safe to assume that your typesetter will understand it and can transpose it into the language of the system he or she is using.

Text Specifications

Whatever system you use, you have to give the typesetter the

---

* Even if you are setting your own type, you should still mark up the copy completely and meticulously.

same set of specifications. For text, the specifications are:

1. The size of the type
2. The amount of linespacing
3. The name of the typeface
4. The font
5. The style
6. The setting
7. The measure

There is an economical coding system for conveying the information. Here is a typical text specification:

10/12 Caledonia, u & lc × 24 pх

The first number tells the typesetter that you want 10 point type. The second adds that you want 2 points of additional linespacing. (Not 12 points. The number after the slash is the cumulative total of the type size and the linespacing or, in other words, the depth of the line.) If you want to set the type solid, simply repeat the first number, 10/10.

Caledonia is the name of the face. Typeface names are always capitalized. Many typefaces are available in different cuts which are usually identified by descriptive names or numbers. Caslon, for instance, comes in Caslon (straight), Caslon Antique, Caslon Old Style, Caslon No. 3, Caslon 540 (a current favorite) and several others. They are all slightly different, and you must include the title or code number, or both, to get the cut you want.

There is no specification for a font in this case. By convention, if you don't specify a font, the typesetter will assume you want the regular roman font, which is the most common for text. If you want something else—italic, boldface, lightface, condensed or extended—you must spell it out in your instructions. (Occasional deviations, such as the odd phrase in italic or boldface are marked independently in the text; your type specifications refer to the bulk of the text.)

"U & lc" is the abbreviation for "upper and lower case" which means that the initial letter of every sentence and every proper noun and adjective will be capitalized. You will rarely set text in any other style, and you don't even have to include this instruction. If you leave it out, the typesetter will assume you want u & lc.

The setting instructions have also been omitted, and the typesetter will understand that the text is to be justified. If you want something else, you have to spell it out.

Finally, you specify the measure; "✕ 24 px" means "on a line 24 picas long". "Picas" may be abbreviated as "pi", "ps", or "px".

If you specified ragged-right text, the specification would look something like this:

10/12 Caledonia, u & lc.
fl l, rag rt, ✕ 24 px max.

With a ragged-right setting, you have to specify a maximum measure, leaving the typesetter to decide where to break the lines short of the maximum. If you want to limit the measure in both directions, you specify a minimum and maximum measure as "✕ 22 px min., 24 px max." or "✕ 22/24 px".

These are the basic parameters. If you have any special instructions to the typesetter, add a semicolon and spell them out. Usually, special instructions refer to spacing parameters ("tight spacing", "automatic kerning" and so on) or to format ("first paragraphs flush out", if you don't want an indent after a head).

Text specifications are written in the left margin of the manuscript opposite the first paragraph to which they apply, and should always be in ink, since the manuscript will be heavily handled; pencil marks may smear or rub off. It is usually a good idea to use a different color from other editorial markings.

If your handwriting isn't as clear as it might be, print the specifications carefully—in caps if necessary. The typesetter is interested in clarity, not calligraphy. Even if you are typesetting the copy yourself, still mark up the copy in the same way. You probably won't remember all the details once you are at the keyboard.

Any segment of the text that deviates from the general specifications must also be marked in the margin.

Lists are usually set in the same face as the main text, but

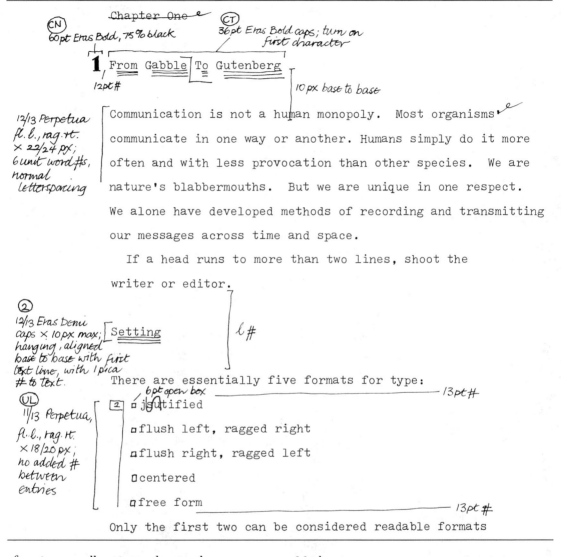

Chapter One

(CN) 60pt Eras Bold, 75% black

(CT) 36pt Eras Bold caps; turn on first character

1 From Gabble To Gutenberg

12pt #

10 px base to base

12/13 Perpetua
fl. l., rag. rt.
× 22/24 px;
6 unit word #s,
normal
letterspacing

Communication is not a human monopoly. Most organisms
communicate in one way or another. Humans simply do it more
often and with less provocation than other species. We are
nature's blabbermouths. But we are unique in one respect.
We alone have developed methods of recording and transmitting
our messages across time and space.

If a head runs to more than two lines, shoot the
writer or editor.

(2)
12/13 Eras Demi
caps × 10px max;
hanging, aligned
base to base with first
text line, with 1 pica
to text.

Setting

l #

(UL)
11/13 Perpetua,
fl. l., rag. rt.
× 18/20 px;
no added #
between
entries

There are essentially five formats for type:

6 pt open box ———————————————— 13pt #

2 □ justified

□ flush left, ragged right

□ flush right, ragged left

□ centered

□ free form ———————————————— 13pt #

Only the first two can be considered readable formats

often in a smaller size and on a shorter measure. Mark up accordingly. You will also need to mark the spacing above and below the list and between the entries, and the amount of indention. Indentions are usually measured in ems, the symbol for which is a square with the number of ems written inside. The right side of the square is extended down the copy to be indented. If you use bullets or quads to lead the entry, they must be specified (in points) with the spacing to follow them.

Two sections of marked-up manuscript. The circled codes (such as the CN for chapter number) were used alone after the first example to save rewriting the specifications in full.

Long quotations are often set a size down from the text but with the same line depth. Again, write out the complete set of specifications, and mark the spacing above and below and the amount of indention.

Footnotes are usually set much smaller than the text with their own linespacing. (Since they are set at the bottom of the page, you don't have to be concerned about alignment.) They are often separated from the text by a rule, which can run part way across the page or to the full measure. If you use a rule, specify its size (in points), its length (in picas), and the spacing above and below.

Display Specifications

Specifications for displays follow the same general rules, but need some extra details:

8. Position

9. Vertical spacing

Displays must be marked up individually, except for text heads. Each level of head (major sectional heads, minor heads, subheads) should be specced the first time it appears and given a code number or letter which can be used thereafter.

Here is a typical specification for a text head:

16 pt Univers bold caps, with
6 pt # above, 4 pt # below

There is no indication of linespacing because I have checked that all of these major heads will fit on one line. There is no measure for the same reason.

If you suspect the heads will have to be turned, you need to add three further specifications: the line spacing, the measure, and the positioning of the turned line. The specification might then look like this:

16/20 Univers bold caps, fl l × 15 px max.,
turned on the first character

I have added a maximum measure, allowing the typesetter to decide where to turn the line, and I have finished with an instruction to set the turned lines flush with the first. If I wanted them indented, I would write something like "turned on the fifth character". I have also dropped the spacing specs because turned heads should usually be set as patches and pasted into position in the mechanical. You can't maintain uniform spacing when some of the heads are on one line and some are on two or three. (Let's say the text with this head is set in 11/13 type. A one-line head won't affect the alignment—$16 + 6 + 4 = 26$ points or two text lines. But a two-line head is $16 + 4$ (linespace) $+ 16$ (second line) $+ 6 + 4$ which does not equal a whole number of 13 point lines.)

Displays may be set in a variety of styles, so you must indicate the style: u & lc, c & lc or caps. (Technically, c & lc means "with initial caps for all major words" although many people do not distinguish between c & lc and u & lc.) For safety, you should mark the text itself, e.g., by underscoring the initial caps three times.

Heads are usually set centered (ctrd), flush left (fl left or fl l), or flush right. Tell the typesetter what you want.

With any form of display other than heads, make a clearly drawn layout on tracing paper and send it to the typesetter with the copy. Trace down the type from a specimen sheet as carefully as you can in the right size and position. A clean layout can save questions and delays.

Proofreading

Even as a designer, you may be called upon to mark up the copy as a whole, and you will certainly be checking proofs. That means you must know, and use, the standard editorial and proofreading symbols as well as the typesetting codes. They are listed with their meanings on Pages 156 and 157.

At the manuscript stage, all corrections and markup (except for the type specifications) are made on the typewritten text itself, which is the reason for double-spaced copy. You need the space above the lines for many corrections.

If a word is incorrectly spelled, run a line through it and write the correct version immediately above. If a character has been left out, insert a caret ($\wedge$) below the space it goes into and write the letter above. Mark all indentions, italics (with a single underscore), boldfaces (with a wavy underscore), dashes ($\frac{1}{m}$) to differentiate them from hyphens, small caps (double underscore) and full caps (triple underscore) if there is any doubt about whether you want caps or not. (Obviously, you don't mark caps at the beginning of sentences, for instance.)

PROOFREADER'S MARKS

In Text	Margin	Meaning	Correction

DELETIONS

In Text	Margin	Meaning	Correction
Bruce Rogers	℘ or ⅋	delete	Bruce Rogers
Bruce Rogers	℘	delete and close up	Bruce Rogers
Bruce Rogers	(stet)	don't change	Bruce Rogers

ADDITIONS

In Text	Margin	Meaning	Correction
Bruc Rogers	e	letter/word	Bruce Rogers
Bruce Rogers	⌃	comma	Bruce Rogers,
Bruce Rogers	;	semicolon	Bruce Rogers;
Bruce Rogers	⊙	colon	Bruce Rogers:
Bruce Rogers	⊙	period	Bruce Rogers.
Bruce Rogers	⌄	apostrophe	Bruce Rogers'
Bruce Rogers	⌄/⌄	quotes	"Bruce Rogers"
Bruce Rogers	=	hyphen	Bruce-Rogers
Bruce Rogers	?	query	Bruce Rogers?
Bruce Rogers	!	exclamation point	Bruce Rogers!
Bruce Rogers	(/)	parens	(Bruce Rogers)
Bruce Rogers	[/]	brackets	[Bruce Rogers]
Bruce Rogers	⊥/M	em-dash	Bruce Rogers—
Bruce Rogers	⊥/N	en-dash	Bruce Rogers–
Bruce Rogers	✱	superior figure	Bruce Rogers*

It is also helpful to the typesetter to delete all end-of-line hyphenations that are not to be typeset; the exceptions would usually be compound-word hyphens that happen to fall at the end of lines. And delete any inappropriate underscores that the typist has inserted from habit; a single underscore means one thing only to the typesetter—set in italic.

In Text	Margin	Meaning	Correction
CORRECTIONS			
(Bruce Rogers)	*rom*	*change to roman*	Bruce Rogers
Bruce Rogers	*ital*	*change to italic*	*Bruce Rogers*
Bruce Rogers	*bf*	*change to boldface*	**Bruce Rogers**
bruce Rogers	*caps*	*change to caps*	Bruce Rogers
BRuce Rogers	*lc*	*change to lowercase*	Bruce Rogers
Bruce Rogers	S.C.	*change to small caps*	BRUCE ROGERS
Bruce Rogers	eq.#	*space evenly*	Bruce Rogers
BruceRogers	#	*add space*	Bruce Rogers
Bruce Rogers	⌒	*reduce space*	Bruce Rogers
Bruce Rogers	⌒	*close up completely*	Bruce Rogers
Bruce Rogers	⌐	*turn line here*	Bruce Rogers
Bruce Rogers	¶	*start new paragraph*	Bruce Rogers
Bruce Rogers	*no* ¶	*run paragraphs together*	Bruce Rogers
Bruce Rogers	(tr)	*transpose letters*	Bruce Rogers
(B) Rogers	(sp)	*spell out*	Bruce Rogers
□Bruce Rogers	□	*indent 1 em*	Bruce Rogers
③Bruce Rogers	③	*indent 3 ems*	Bruce Rogers
⌐Rogers⌐	⌐⌐	*center*	Rogers
⌐ Bruce Rogers	⌐	*move flush left*	Bruce Rogers
Bruce Rogers⌐	⌐	*move flush right*	Bruce Rogers
Bruce Rogers	‖	*align vertically*	Bruce Rogers
Bruce Rogers	=	*align horizontally*	Bruce Rogers

Proofs are marked up differently. There is seldom room for instructions in typeset copy. Instructions are written in the right-hand margin; symbols only are written in the text itself, i.e., the marks in the first column in the table above. If there are several corrections on the same line, write the directions in the margin in the same order as the errors in the line, separating them with slashes. And write everything in pencil, not in ink, in case you make a mistake and need to erase it. Every proofreader (and there should always be more than one) should use a different color so you know who made which corrections.

There are, as usual, some tricks of the trade.

First, circle any marginal instructions that are words or abbreviations. The typesetter may assume that any uncircled characters are to be inserted somewhere in the text.

Second, always circle periods and colons in the margin. It is very easy for the typesetter to miss a small dot or pair of dots.

Third, if you are inserting a lower-case ell, write a looped "ℓ" to distinguish it from a numeral "one". Similarly, triple underscore cap O's so they are not confused with lower-case o's, and always write "zero" (circled) next to the numeral 0 to differentiate it from an O.

Fourth, if several words have been transposed, number them in the correct order and write in the margin "set as numbered"; don't use the regular transposition mark. Similarly, if several characters have been garbled, it is simpler to delete the word and reset it completely.

Finally, never try to correct type proof by yourself. It is almost impossible to catch errors if you have to switch continually between marked manuscript and type proof. Persuade somebody else to read the manuscript to you so that you can concentrate on the type. And proof everything—heads, folios and all. It is amazing how many proofreaders skip over heads.

If the type has been photoset, corrections will usually be made and stripped into the film physically. That is good news and bad news. The good news is that you don't have to re-read the entire corrected proof. Anything that was correct the first time will remain correct. On the other hand, the typesetter may have reset several lines of copy even though only one was incorrect. You should proofread several lines ahead of and behind the corrected lines to make sure no new errors have crept in. You should also check that the corrections have been made in exactly the same type as the original version. If you notice variations in the density or sharpness of the type, query the typesetter. Check also for alignment; in photosetting, the stripped-in corrections are sometimes misaligned.

ok/ak Ⓢⓜ

PRENTICE-HALL: A Guide to Type Design JOB$5 1077$$$$6 08-07-84 Galley 36

Don't try to 'design every page of type throughout a book, /⌄

or work it over too carfully after the style is chosen; leave /e

something to accident, so long as it is not a glaring defget. /tr

The proof-reader and the workman in the shop, if they have

been properly instructed, usually may be trusted to take care

of the ordinary details of arrangement. you must, however, /cap

guard against their tendency to bring out all the final lines

of a paragraph or a page to full measure, for many printers

want everything squared up and tidy. THis is the emergence /lc

again of the mechanical faculty, and some proof-readers have

been known to go over every page with a magnifying glass

to be sure there is not the least imperfection in any of the

letters. This is the acme of fastidiousness and is carrying

perfection too far. The use of old or worn types is naturally

not to be recommended, but the habit of too meticulous at- /⌒

tention to every minor detail is apt to result in preciousness,

*Corrected galleys with the top corner initialed to show that the galleys have
been proofread and to identify the proofreader.*

Digitally set corrections will not be misaligned, but are prone
to the same errors as photoset corrections. Justification can
change in odd ways. Proofread as you would for photoset.

There is also a simple trick for proofreading accurately. We
miss (and make) typographic errors mainly because we read and
write in a flow. Consequently, we are apt to see what we ex-
pect to see, rather than what is actually there. Accurate proof-
reading demands that every word be scanned individually and in
isolation from the context. The easiest way to isolate the lines is
to cover the copy with a sheet of blank typing paper and move

it slowly down, reading one line at a time. When you reach the bottom, reverse the process and check for correct word-breaks and hyphenation. If you use this system, it will take you slightly longer to read the text, but you will catch all (or almost all) of the typos. You will rarely do so if you simply scan the text.

One final point, which has more to do with professional courtesy than design per se. Errors made by the typesetter are called printer's errors, or pe's, and they are corrected at the typesetter's expense. Any changes you make are called author's alterations, or AA's (even if you had nothing to do with the writing—but then the typesetter has nothing to do with the printing, either). Some people keep a meticulous scorecard, and religiously identify the pe's on the proof. However, if the pe's are few—and with a good typesetter, they are astonishingly few—I would tend to ignore them in the interests of building a harmonious relationship. There will be innumerable occasions when the typesetter will bail you out and cover your mistakes.

Of course, if the typesetter has mangled the job, by all means charge back the pe's. You will probably not want to work with that firm again.

5 TYPE TECHNOLOGY

Few industries have been as profoundly affected by the electronic revolution as the print business.

For the first four hundred years and more, typesetting and printing methods changed little in substance. If Gutenberg had been able to walk into a typesetting shop in 1860, he would not have found a great deal to surprise him.

Since about 1960, however, typesetting technology has been transformed and is still changing. Where it will be a year or five years from now is anybody's guess. But to get a feeling for where we are now, we have to go back to the beginning.

HAND TYPESETTING

In the system perfected by Gutenberg, characters were cast one by one and stored in cases until they were needed. Gutenberg made matrixes for well over two hundred characters and cast perhaps as many as 50,000 characters for his famous Bible.

The cases originally held a single font of upper- or lower-case characters. Eventually, they were amalgamated into a single case, known in this country as the California case.

The characters were assembled by hand, one by one, line by line, in a device known as a printer's stick, which had a movable flange that could be adjusted to different line lengths. The stick would hold up to about a dozen lines of text type. When it was full, the type was emptied into a galley and the cycle repeated.

By about 1850, a journeyman typesetter had to be able to set 1,000 characters per hour over an average 10-hour day, according to a set of standards published by the union. A master type-

The California case holds several hundred characters of a single font of type

setter might be able to double that output, but in all likelihood it represents the level of output that had prevailed for many centuries.

When all the type was set, it was inked, proofed, corrected and then broken up into pages and transferred to the press. This mode of printing directly from type—letterpress, as it is called—was also as old as Gutenberg, and remained the primary printing process until well into this century.

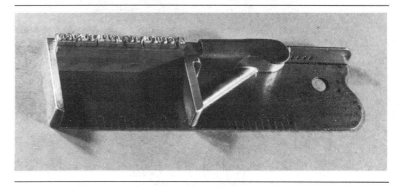

The composing stick, in which a hand typesetter assembled type, held up to a dozen-or-so lines of text type. The movable stop on the left could be shifted to the specified measure and then locked to hold the type firmly in place.

At the end of the press run, the type was cleaned and re-turned to the cases, or, if another printing or edition was planned, stored as standing type. (Whole books were stored this way, tying up a fair amount of the typesetter's supply of raw material.)

The process, by modern standards, was unbelievably cumber-some and slow. It still had one advantage over the systems that succeeded it—the long apprenticeship that produced a fully trained typesetter with a distinct sense of craft. It may have been that sense of craft that postponed the mechanization of typesetting until almost the end of the nineteenth century.

In 1872, an 18-year-old German immigrant, Ottmar Mergen-thaler, arrived in Washington, D.C., and subsequently moved to Baltimore, where he became interested in typesetting machines. At that time, a number of mechanical systems had been pro-posed and patented, but none had proved itself commercially. However, Mergenthaler introduced a new machine, the Lino-type, in 1884, and it was successfully demonstrated two years later at the *New York Tribune*.

MECHANIZED TYPESETTING

It was to become a predominant system until well after World War II.

The Linotype is actually a combined typecaster and typeset-ter, and that was the key to its success. It has three major com-ponents: a magazine containing the matrixes, or type molds, a keyboard and a casting mechanism.

The magazine is a large flat case containing 90 channels in which the matrixes are stored. The matrixes carry a single mold, or a pair of molds for related fonts (say, the roman and italic), so the magazine holds two complete fonts. A second magazine can be attached, giving the system a capacity of four fonts.

The matrixes are released by the operator's keystrokes and assembled in a line. Instead of blank quads, however, long, flexi-ble wedges called space bands are inserted between the words. When the line is almost full, the operator pulls a lever, the space bands are pushed in to fill out the line, and the matrixes are carried to the casting mechanism, where molten type metal is forced into the molds to make a line of type in a single slug. Meanwhile the operator continues to type.

The Linotype machine. The magazine is at the top of the machine above the keyboard, with the control bar, which redistributed the matrixes into the right channels, over it. The casting system is to the left of the keyboard, behind the slanted galley into which the type slugs were ejected.

A line of matrixes with the space bands, which were forced into the wordspaces to justify the line.

After the line has been cooled, it is ejected into a galley while the matrixes are returned to their proper channels to be recycled. (Each matrix has a unique set of notches in the bottom which correspond to the opening in the top of the channel, so there is no danger that a matrix will find its way into the wrong channel. Handset type was always in danger of being mixed, or pi-ed.)

Mechanization brought an exponential increase in speed. Because the operator can type almost without interruption, the system is capable of setting about 6,000 characters per hour. And, for the first time, fonts could be mixed directly and instantaneously; in hand typesetting, one set of cases had to be returned to storage and a new set hauled out for a change of font. Moreover, the typesetter had to keep only the magazines, instead of hundreds of typecases. And the type metal could always be cleaned and reused.

One major disadvantage of the system was that a single correction still meant recasting a whole line. It was also less suitable for setting displays, which were usually handset until the advent in 1906 of the Ludlow system, a semi-mechanized display typesetter.

Linotype was so successful that in 1912, when the early patents lapsed, a very similar machine, the Intertype, was introduced by the International Typesetting Machine Company. There really is nothing to choose between the two systems.

However, a few years after Linotype's successful debut, an entirely different mechanical system was patented by Tolbert Lanston, a former lawyer from Troy, New York.

Lanston's Monotype has two independent mechanisms: a keyboard and a typecaster. On the keyboard, the operator produces a punched paper tape on which the text and design specifications are coded as rows of holes, something like a pianola roll. This tape drives the typecaster.

The Monotype matrixes are held in a rectangular frame, which can accommodate up to 255 of them. On command from the tape, the frame moves to position a matrix at the opening of the casting pot, from which molten metal is forced into the mold. The character is then water-cooled and dropped into a channel holding a line of type, which is ejected into a galley when the line is full.

The caster can produce from about 3,300 24-point characters to nearly 11,000 5-point characters an hour, but, taking everything into consideration, it is generally slightly slower than the Linotype. One the other hand, it holds a greater number of matrixes, which can include a variety of special sorts. Correction is also somewhat faster and easier since the characters are cast individually and can be replaced one at a time.

All in all, however, both systems were equally efficient. Newspaper and magazine publishers tended to prefer the Linotype because of its speed. Book publishers liked the Monotype for its versatility and the high quality of its faces. (In the early years of this century, Monotype launched an ambitious program to recut and revive many of the classic typefaces, under the direction of Stanley Morison, one of the greatest modern typographers.)

The Monotype keyboarding machine. The punched paper tape that operated the typecaster is at the top, directly above the dual keyboards.

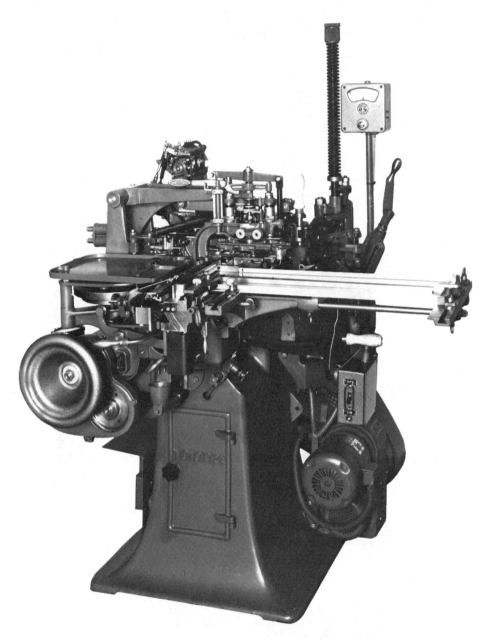

The Monotype typecaster. The tape was mounted into the feed mechanism sticking up at left. The matrix case was held by the complex system at center, which moved it into position over the casting pot. The characters were ejected into the long galley sticking out to the right.

It is hardly surprising that Linotype and Monotype between them rang the death knell of hand typesetting, which was largely relegated to the contradictory roles of fine bookwork and job typesetting.

They remained the dominant technologies until the 1960s, when they were successfully challenged by a revolutionary new system of typesetting: phototypesetting.

The half-millenium that ended in the 1950s was the era of metal type. It is sometimes referred to as the era of hot-metal type, a phrase that I have always found slightly silly. Nobody actually used hot metal type except by accident.

COLD TYPESETTING

Since the 1950s, the use of metal type has declined steadily, and it has been replaced by other systems, known equally fatuously as cold-type systems, that do not, with one exception, use metal type.

The exception is an offshoot of a technology older than Linotype—the typewriter. Regular typewriters are not, in any real sense, typesetting systems, despite their name. They generally have only one face, and they do not space characters differentially. Nor are their products meant to be reproduced in large quantities. They are mechanical writing machines.

Since the 1950s, however, several manufacturers have brought out sophisticated typewriters capable of letterspacing and supplied with interchangeable type fonts. They are known collectively as strike-on systems.

The oldest is the Varityper. Varityper fonts are curved metal strips on which the characters are embossed. Two of these 99-character fonts can be mounted at the same time. The machine, which is essentially an electric typewriter with some additional keys, can linespace in half-point increments and set horizontal and vertical rules. It produces what is, in effect, a repro proof which can be pasted directly into a mechanical.

Varityper produces a respectable facsimile of type, and some 1,600 fonts are available. The chief drawback is that the copy must be keyboarded twice for justified copy; the first time to enter the text, and the second, to adjust the wordspacing. Changing fonts can also be a time-consuming process.

IBM has two strike-on systems. The basic system is the Selectric Composer, which is comparable to the Varityper. Fonts are mounted on the familiar IBM ball, one at a time, although they can be interchanged quickly. The more sophisticated system combines a Composer and a modified typewriter. The typewriter produces a magnetic tape on which the text and design specifications are encoded, and a parallel paper copy for proofing. The tape can be corrected and then transferred to a microcomputer which drives the Composer at a speed of about 150 justified words per minute. However, the operator must stand by to hyphenate and change fonts.

Strike-on systems are comparatively inexpensive, and turn out a product that the most readers cannot distinguish from the genuine typeset article. They are, however, comparatively slow, and corrections can be even slower; whole pages must be re-typed or corrected copy cut and pasted into position. They are also restricted to text sizes. The IBM systems have another concealed hazard for the designer accustomed to type; fonts come in only three arbitrary alphabet lengths (all 6–8 point fonts are the same length, as are the 9–10 point fonts, and the 11–12 point fonts).

There is another inexpensive cold-type system that can provide display type for strike-on systems. It is known generically as transfer type or press type. Press type is printed on acetate sheets with a tacky backing. The character may be cut out and transferred to the layout or burnished through the acetate onto the sheet below. Cut-out letters can be picked up and repositioned; burnished letters must be removed and replaced. (The only safe method is to lift them with masking tape. If you try to scrape off or erase dry-transfer type, you will generally make a mess of it.) Both types must be given a final firm burnishing to mount them permanently.

Transfer type is available in innumerable faces, and many of the manufacturers commission or purchase new faces every year—some of dubious value. By shopping around, however, you can find some quite obscure faces that typesetters rarely carry. You can also find symbols, rules, dingbats, and an array of unimaginative, but professionally rendered, graphics.

The chief drawbacks to transfer type are that it is a laborious medium, particularly if there is any appreciable amount of copy to set, and that it takes a certain amount of dexterity and experience to produce a passable result.

Obviously, strike-on and transfer type do not offer a serious threat to the established typesetting systems although they have proved their worth for the tight-budgeted.

Phototypesetting, on the other hand, has all but eliminated metal typesetting.

The first photo systems appeared in the 1930s, but they were generally regarded as a curiosity rather than a serious technology. However, they were based on a revolutionary new principle; they produced type images directly from a photographic negative, printed on film or photosensitive paper. The type image could be manipulated like any other photographic image. Photo type could be curved, twisted, arched, diminished in perspective or run through just about any other hoop an art director or designer could dream up. Almost inevitably, the advertising industry took phototypesetting to its heart. Few others did at first.

By the end of the 1950s, however, the demand for type had increased enormously, and there was a growing demand for greater versatility that the metal typesetting systems could not meet. They had reached an ultimate level of perfection, but they had also reached their limits of speed and flexibility.

The major manufacturers attempted to meet the challenge by installing film matrixes in their machines, but the systems were still restricted to operating at mechanical speeds. They were quickly supplanted by a second generation of true phototypesetting systems which now dominate the field. Over a hundred of these systems are offered currently by a dozen or so manufacturers.

Although the systems vary in capacity and detail, they all operate on the same fundamental principles. Text and design specifications are encoded at a keyboard on magnetic or punched paper tape or entered directly from a video display terminal. The tape may be used to drive the typesetting mechanism directly, or passed through a computer for hyphenation and justification first.

The heart of the typesetter is the image master which holds the film matrixes, in the form of photographic negatives. Image masters may be film strips, drums, glass or plastic discs, or grids similar to the Monotype grid.

They are mounted in front of a high-intensity light source that flashes on command from the tape at precisely timed intervals, as the appropriate character comes into position. The beam may then pass through a lens system which reduces or enlarges

Mergenthaler's compact V-I-P phototypesetter is one of the most widely used in commercial typesetting. It is operated by a punched paper tape, which can be seen looped in front, produced on a separate keyboard system. Up to 18 image masters can be mounted at the same time to produce type from 6 point to 72 point at a rate of 50 newspaper lines per minute.

172

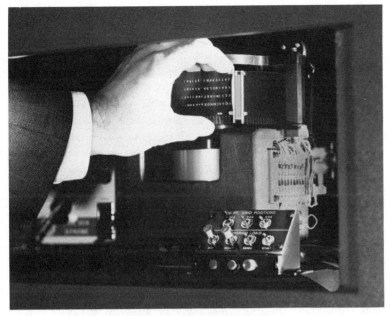

The V-I-P font grid is simply a film strip that can be attached or removed in seconds. About a thousand typefaces are available for the system.

the image to the correct point size. From there, it passes through a set of prisms to strike a strip of film or photosensitive paper, creating lines of latent type images that appear when the film is developed.

Photosystems are far faster than mechanized systems because they are not obliged to cast metal and because, apart from the image master and the prism system, they contain no moving parts. The more sophisticated systems can set up to 4,500 characters a minute in as many as 18 different fonts, ranging in size from 3.5 points to 72 points. Smaller systems operate at slower speeds and cannot mount as many fonts at one time, but they are comparable in cost to office duplicating machines.

Although many systems are capable of setting large type sizes, displays are more often set on specialized photolettering or photodisplay machines. These operate on the same general principles, but at much slower speeds. They set one character at a time, but allow the operator to position and space the characters very precisely. Many systems set only one line at a time, although several are capable of setting consecutive lines. On the other hand they are also capable of manipulating the images through anamorphic lenses into a dazzling array of effects.

The high speed of phototypesetting systems and the versatility of photodisplay systems make them far more economical than their mechanized counterparts. Keyboarding is one uninterrupted process, since end-of-line decisions are almost universally left to the computer. The type is set at exponentially higher speeds, and many more fonts are available in the machine. Some systems produce the full range of sizes from a single image master by projecting the image through magnifying or reducing lenses.

The machines are also compact and take up comparatively little room; image masters have replaced the far more bulky Linotype and Monotype matrix magazines. A typesetter can now store thousands of fonts in something comparable in size to a three-drawer filing cabinet.

Corrections can be made inexpensively at several points in the system. Paper copy can be produced from the tape for proofreading before a single character is set, and the tape corrected simply by merging with a correction tape. Many keyboards are also equipped with visual display units, so that the operator can correct while keyboarding.

Moreover, the film produced by the machine can be sent to the printer to be used directly to make the printing plate. Several expensive intermediate processes can be cut out, and the printed product is superior because it is only one generation away from the original.

However, phototypesetting has also produced its share of headaches.

Few designers who have worked with metal type would disagree that the general quality of typesetting has deteriorated. Many of the experienced typesetters who operated the mechanical systems could not or would not change over to the new technology. As a result, a long tradition of craft stretching back to Gutenberg was broken, and a irreplaceable pool of skill disappeared. The new typesetters had to learn their trade from the ground up, without the benefit of an apprenticeship, on unfamiliar equipment that had no precedents or models.

The manufacturers compounded the problem unwittingly by making progressively more-foolproof equipment. Today, virtually anyone who can type can be trained in a matter of days to operate a simple typesetting system. And, while it is difficult to blame typesetters for hiring such operators, there is a great deal more to typesetting than accurate keyboarding. No matter how tight your specifications, you still depend on the typesetter for many critical judgements, which few of the current generation of typesetters have been trained to make.

The manufacturers have also produced a plethora of typefaces designed to be used exclusively on their own equipment. Some are proprietary versions of the standard faces, all too often pale shadows of the originals. Worse still, they all tend to differ slightly, but significantly. As a result, the designer must relearn the characteristics of familiar faces with every change of system.

Moreover, these redesigned faces are usually renamed, adding to the confusion. That old workhorse Helvetica now parades under AG Book, Claro, Geneva, Helvetstar, Megaron, Vega and probably half a dozen other pseudonyms that I have not yet run across.

Lack of expertise and competitive pressure have also led to the abandonment of many typographic refinements. Perhaps the most distressing is the use of a single master for many point sizes. Eight-point type is not simply a miniature duplicate of 14 point type. The designers of metal faces understood the optical adjustments that are required as type is reduced or enlarged and redesigned the fonts to account for the differences. For example, smaller sizes need more open counters, thinner stems, more extended letter-forms and more-open letterspacing if they are to appear consistent with the larger sizes. When all sizes come from a single matrix, however, it is impossible to compensate for the visual differences.

These are purely esthetic concerns, but there are some practical hazards to be guarded against if you are dealing with phototype.

We have already discussed the problems of computerized H&J programs and misaligned corrections.

If your type is set on stabilization paper, rather than film or photographic paper, the image will gradually fade. Avoid stabilization paper if the mechanical is to be reused. After several months, the type may have to be reset.

Check your proofs for variations in the density of the image.

175

AB AB
AB AB
abc abc
abc abc

8 point and 14 point characters magnified to the same size. The difference in the weighting of the metal characters at left is obvious. The 8 point digital type at right, in contrast, is simply a small version of the 14 point, made from the same matrix. Metal type designs were usually produced in three modified versions: for the smaller type sizes, text faces, and display faces.

If the typesetter does not control focus, exposure, development time and other factors carefully, the quality of the image can deteriorate considerably. Make sure that corrections are set on the same equipment under precisely the same conditions as the original. For example, if your original is a 10 point type made from a 10 point master, it will look very different from corrections in a 10 point type reduced from a 14 point master.

Finally, check that all the faces you intend to use are aligned uniformly. Most systems now align on the baseline, but some older models use faces that may be aligned on the center or top-aligned. Differently aligned faces are not compatible with one another.

Depite these criticisms, there is no disputing that phototypesetting has proved itself. However, its dominance may be short-lived. A new, and even more versatile technology is challenging it for supremacy.

Once computers enter the picture, they have a habit of taking over. Computers entered typesetting originally to relieve operators of the time-consuming end-of-line decisions. By the 1970s, however, they had begun to take over the typesetting process itself. They have now reached a remarkable level of sophistication and will almost certainly make other typesetting systems obsolete.

The earliest digital typesetters were adaptations of the second-generation phototypesetters. They are generally known as photo/scan cathode ray tube (CRT) systems. They still employ film image masters as matrixes, but the image is scanned onto a cathode ray tube, like the picture tube in your television set, by a computer-controlled beam. The image is formed electronically on the face of the tube as a series of dots or fine vertical scanlines. From there it is projected onto film or photosensitive paper. The result is a considerable increase in speed, since the system is now operating essentially at the rate of a computer.

Within a few years, a more advanced type of system, the digital/scan CRT system, appeared. This is a purely computerized system. Fonts are stored as strings of digital commands which control the beam projecting onto the CRT screen. The commands may reproduce a standard face, or they may simply define components of characters—stems, curves, serifs, and so on—that can be assembled into standard faces or entirely original faces. Characters can be manipulated at will before they are transmitted to the screen; for example, you can create a large x-height Garamond with a few keystrokes or a set of swash italics for Univers 56 if the mood strikes you.

More recently, an even more sophisticated type of digital system has appeared—the digital/laser system—in which a laser beam forms characters directly onto film, photosensitive paper or even a printing plate at phenomenal speed. The larger systems can scan an average of 20,000 characters per minute, and the more powerful systems range up to 90,000 characters per minute or 1,500 characters per second. The characters are formed by overlapping scan lines, with more than 1,600 lines to the inch. They may well be the crispest images ever created by any typesetting system. Moreover, hundreds of 100–180 character fonts can be stored in the system, with up to 200 on line at any time. Fonts can also be changed with a few keystrokes.

Computerized Typesetting

The Compugraphic MCS 8400 is a state-of-the-art digital photo/scan typesetter. It operates with 16 fonts on line, stored on 8-inch floppy disks that can be changed in seconds. It produces 150 lines of type per minute in sizes from 5 point to 72 point on measures up to 70 picas. The characters can be expanded, condensed, slanted in either direction, and reversed.

The MCS 20 is the front end for the MCS 8400. Essentially, it is an extremely versatile word-processor. The components of the system are a 128 kilobyte control unit (out of sight below the keyboard operator), which stores the operating programs, a double-disk drive for the user's system programs and data, a VDT and a keyboard. The entire system can be kept on a console no larger than the average office desk.

179

The keyboard of the MCS 20. The standard alphanumeric keys also control design specification when used in combination with the first of the white user definable keys in the row above. The other keys in this row can be programmed by the operator. The last four change point size, measure, linespacing and type font instantaneously. The keypads to the left and right control editing and file management functions for word-processing.

Type sizes range from 4 point to 120 point and the type can be set on measures up to 70 picas, in virtually any page or tabular format.

The system is controlled from a word-processor on which the text can be entered, edited and corrected and the design codes inserted. The smaller CRT systems, known as direct-entry systems, are in effect word-processors that output a typeset, instead of a typewritten, product.

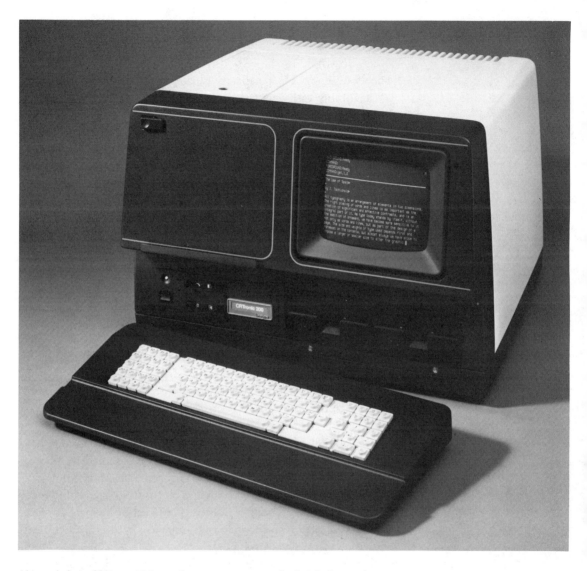

Mergenthaler's CRTronic200 is a direct entry system only slightly larger than an office typewriter. Despite its compactness, it has 24 fonts on line that can be set in sizes from 4 point to 128 point in tenth-of-an-inch increments, at a rate of 125 lines per minute. It will also slant, condense, expand and reverse type and set rules and borders.

The larger systems can accept data from a number of sources simultaneously—word-processing terminals, computers, and other electronic media—by direct cable connections or over telephone lines. Their capacity obviously is far beyond the capacity of any one operator, and they may be linked with visual layout, or page make-up, systems capable of even more complex layouts, including complicated contouring.

Perhaps the most surprising feature of CRT and digital laser systems is their cost. The larger systems are comparable in price to other main-frame computers, but direct-entry systems can be bought for less than $25,000, and manufacturers are predicting steady decreases in price.

It would seem that we have reached the ultimate state of the art in typesetting. However, more advances are to come. Some manufacturers are already developing voice-controlled systems and further improvements in computer memories will increase the capacity of the systems far beyond the current level.

Moreover, the first generation of computerized printers, the laser/jet systems, is now reaching the market. These operate at speeds comparable to the digital/laser typesetters and are capable of scanning-in all forms of artwork, black-and-white and color, directly. In other words, the entire print process, from the word-processor that accepts the original copy to the jet printer that produces the finished product, has been digitized.

Virtually all of the hackwork and the mechanical chores that were once part-and-parcel of print has been assumed by the computer. Only one thing has not changed; the process must still be initiated by a human mind. The most striking difference will be that the controlling human mind will be free to do what it does best, to create, largely untrammeled by the need to deal with rote mechanical problems.

In a sense, we may have come full circle in print. The cycle began with the versatile scholar/printers who produced their own basic materials, deployed them, and produced the books that changed western history. We will need equally versatile individuals to continue the process in the decades ahead—generalists who can write, edit, design and execute through the medium of the computer.

Gutenberg—to parody the old bumper sticker—seems to be alive and well and living in Silicon Valley.

One segment of the print industry has so far remained fairly immune to the electronic revolution. Papermaking, in some respects the oldest branch, is still essentially a craft.

Papermaking may seem remote from design in other ways, but the products of both processes coincide critically. The weight, finish and other characteristics of the paper you use will influence the appearance of your type.

There are many grades and types of paper, but only three—book papers, writing papers, and cover papers—are of immediate interest to the designer. Cover papers, as the name implies, are stiffer papers used to print the covers of booklets, brochures, annual reports, paperback books and the like. Writing papers include typing and correspondence papers and duplicating papers for office machines. Book papers are used for practically everything else we read, and they are of prime concern to the designer.

The subject of paper is steeped in a jargon as esoteric as type talk, but you need only a small vocabulary to make your wants known.

When you are selecting a paper, probably the first thing you think about is its weight, or, more properly, basis weight.

The basis weight of a paper is the weight (in pounds) of a ream (500 sheets) of a standard size sheet. With the perversity typical of everything connected with type, standard size differs with the type of paper. For book papers, it is $25'' \times 38''$; for cover stock, it is $20'' \times 26''$; and for writing papers, it is $17'' \times 22''$.

Then, to make things more confusing, paper is sold in double reams, or 1,000-sheet lots. A 50lb book paper, for instance, will appear on the bill priced at so much for a 25×38—100M which translates into a book sheet (the standard size) weighing 100lb per thousand sheets (M is the papermaker's abbreviation for "thousand"). If you remember that, you won't panic.

Book papers come in ten basis weights; 30lb, 40lb, 45lb, 50lb, 60lb, 70lb, 80lb, 90lb, 100lb, and 120lb. (I have never been able to figure out what happened to 110lb paper.)

Generally speaking, the heavier the paper, the stiffer, thicker and more opaque the sheet. Books are generally printed on 40–80lb papers which will stand up to a fair amount of wear and tear. Glossier products may be printed on heavier stocks so that they will feel more substantial. Ephemeral products can be printed on lighter papers, which generally cost less.

A more accurate guide to the thickness of the paper, however, is the caliper. The caliper is the thickness of four sheets in thousandths of an inch (or points, as papermakers call them, just to confuse everybody else). Another measure, used mostly in book publishing, is the bulk, which is measured in pages per inch (PPI). Publishers will often choose a high bulking paper to beef up the heft of a book, particularly if the text is fairly short and the price is fairly high. On the other hand, if you have a very long text that might scare off the reader, you can create a less weighty impression by printing on a less bulky paper. You have to remember, however, that the lower the bulk, the higher the number of pages per inch.

Opacity is another vital factor to consider. Opacity is an index of the amount of light that penetrates the paper (the visual opacity) or the depth to which it absorbs ink (the printing opacity). The two are quite different. A paper may have a relatively low visual capacity, because the sheet is thin, but a high printing opacity, because the surface has been treated so that the ink does not sink in. Both indices are important to the designer.

Printed opacity tells you whether the printing on the back side of the sheet will show through on the front; visual opacity tells you whether the printing on the next page will show through. In a book, you generally want neither. In a flyer, which will only be read once and discarded, you would probably accept some show-through in the interests of cost. Opaque papers are generally more expensive. Again, if the product is heavily illustrated, you need a high printed opacity, so that half-tones do not show through and interfere with the clarity of the type on the other side of the sheet.

But perhaps the most important characteristic for the designer is finish. Finish determines the kinds of things you can and cannot print on the paper.

Book papers can be divided into two major categories of finish: coated and uncoated. The major difference between them is that coated stocks have been specially processed to absorb little or no ink.

There are five grades of uncoated papers.

Antique papers have the roughest surface and generally the highest bulk. They are the cheapest book papers. They are essentially designed to print text and line art; halftones tend to blur because the unfinished surface absorbs ink unevenly. The rough finish, however, is similar to the finish of handmade papers, so they are very much at home with oldstyles and transitionals. In fact, the only family that does not show up well on an antique paper is the moderns, which generally need a smoother surface.

Eggshell papers, as the name implies, have a slightly smoother finish and lower bulk, but they are used in much the same way as antiques.

Machine-finish papers have been calendered, or smoothed between polished steel rollers. Consequently, they have a smooth surface that will accept medium-screen halftones, as well as text and line art. However, the two sides of the sheet are slightly different; the wire-side, which was in contact with the mesh of the papermaking machine, is slightly rougher than the felt-side, or upper side. In the cheaper grades of machine-finish, you may have to take the difference into account if you are printing halftones or color.

Machine-finishes are widely used for magazines and longer books because the smoother finish gives them a lower bulk.

The two smoothest unfinished stocks, English finish and super-calendered, are becoming less common because they are often more expensive than the cheaper grades of coated stock. English finish is made with clay fillers (originally imported from England) to produce a smooth surface that does not absorb ink readily. Supercalendered papers are given a second calendering on ultrasmooth rollers that produce the smoothest finish possible in uncoated stocks. Both of these grades reproduce the finest halftones beautifully.

However, coated stocks do the job even better. As the name implies, coated papers are covered with a layer of fine clay, which is supercalendered to the surface. This layer prevents the ink from penetrating to the paper fibers so that it lies on the surface of the paper, producing a very dense image.

Film-coated paper is the least expensive grade. The coating is applied in the papermaking machine, so that the surface is less brilliant than the more expensive grades. However, the lower reflectivity is an asset; flat colors and halftones can be combined with text, which is more difficult to read on the brighter coated papers.

Conversion-coated papers are given a wash-coating like film-coated paper, but a second, higher-quality coating is applied later. This surface can be treated to leave a matt or glossy finish, both of which are ideal for process color. Conversion-coated papers are commonly used for reproductions of fine art and high-quality photography.

Blade-coated papers also receive a double-coating, the second being a viscous pigment that dries to a matt finish, which is less wearing on the eye when text is combined with illustrations.

The highest grade of coated paper, cast-coated, is so expensive to produce that it is made in single sheets, often to order. It is used only for the most expensive items, such as covers for presentation pieces and the glossiest of annual reports.

Both categories of papers may be waterproofed for use on offset presses, in which case they are known—sensibly, for once—as offset papers.

The cheaper grades of uncoated paper are made in a wide variety of colors. All grades of paper are made in white. However, we have to be careful of the term "white" when it comes to paper. Coated papers are pure white, which makes many of them less suitable for printing text; the intense contrast between black type and pure white paper is fatiguing to the eye.

Uncoated stocks, on the other hand are made in a wide range of off-whites, none of which is pure white. You can find anything from a warm cream to a cold blue-white. Generally, you can't detect the difference unless you compare the papers directly. However, the small shifts in color can have a staggering effect on the appearance of the type. Bodoni on a warm white paper loses some of its aloofness; Caslon on a cold white develops an uncharacteristic glitter. Futura becomes almost human on a cream-colored stock, and all the monoweights become sharper and crisper on the cooler whites.

It takes experience to predict the effect that a paper will have on your design. Sometimes, however, you can persuade the typesetter to run a sample on the paper you have selected.

Your choice will usually be dictated by the papers your printer keeps in stock. If you want something different, the printer will usually acquire it for you, but at a price. To begin with, in any case, you are probably better off picking something from the printer's collection of swatches. And, until you have a firm grasp of the subject, it is usually smart to tell the printer what you want and follow his or her advice.

At the very worst, you will be able to order your paper in language that the printer will understand, and—who knows?—you may even be able to fool some people into believing you are an expert. After all, an expert is just a damn fool with a briefcase and a collection of jargon five miles from home.

A COPYFITTING

Copyfitting, or copycasting, means calculating the area that your copy will take up when it is converted into type.

There are several methods of copyfitting, some more precise than others. However, the shorter the copy, the more accurate the calculations must be. In a book-length manuscript, you can work with averages because there is more leeway to compensate for errors when you make up the dummy for the printer. For a three-fold flyer, on the other hand, your calculations must be exact; there is no room for mistakes.

Unless the copy has been written to fit the design, it is usually smart to copyfit the manuscript before you start planning the design. There is not much point in producing a prize-winning design plan, only to find that the copy runs fifty lines longer (or shorter) than the space you've allowed for it.

No matter which copyfitting method you use, there are three steps to the process:

1. Casting off, or computing the number of characters in the original copy

2. Calculating the number of lines of type represented by the cast-off

3. Calculating the depth of the text block.

You follow the steps in this order unless you are working from a fixed layout, such as a magazine master layout, in which case you reverse the steps.

CASTING OFF   In copyfitting, every letter, numeral, punctuation mark and
wordspace is considered a character.

If the copy has been word-processed, the cast-off is simple.
The keystrokes, by and large, are equivalent to the character
count, and they will be recorded by the word-processor itself.
However, you must remember to subtract about 1 percent of
the total to account for formatting commands that will not be
typeset (e.g., "hard" returns to end paragraphs or insert line
spaces).

Simpler word-processors, such as personal computers, often
don't keep a running count of the keystrokes, but the cast-off
can be made from the floppy disks. When you list the files on
the disk, the system will tell you the amount of space used (or
remaining, which amounts to the same thing). A standard, double-density 5¼″ disk holds about 180,000 characters, so a simple calculation will convert the percentage of space taken up by
the copy into a cast-off. Again, remember to subtract 1 percent
for format commands.

If you are dealing with old-fashioned, hard copy, pounded
out on a typewriter, you have to do some old-fashioned—but
not particularly hard—manual calculations.

The quick-and-dirty method, which should be used only with
longer manuscripts, is to find the average length of the typewritten line by sampling several pages, and multiplying the result by the number of lines in the copy.

A more precise method involves several steps.

First, find the shortest full line on each page, ignoring short,
end-of-paragraph lines. Then draw a vertical line through the
copy in the letterspace at the end of this line, as shown opposite.

Count the number of characters in the short line and multi-
ply the result by the number of lines on the page.

Next, count the "left-over" characters to the right of the
cut-off line, and add that total to your first total. However, you
must add a character to every line ending with a complete
word. When the copy is typeset, the word will be followed by a
wordspace, which, obviously, you can't see in the typewritten
version. If you forget to account for the "invisible" wordspaces,
your count will be off by about 25 characters per page.

Ignore end-of-line hyphens; the same words will probably not
be broken and hyphenated when the copy is typeset. It is usu-

If the copy has been word-processed, the cast-off is simple. The keystrokes, by and large, are equivalent to the character count, and they will be recorded by the word-processor itself. However, you must remember to subtract about 1 percent of the total to account for formatting commands that will not be typeset (e.g., "hard returns" to end paragraphs or insert line spaces).

careful! this is an end-of-paragraph line

Simpler word-processors, such as personal computers, often do don't keep a running count of keystrokes, but the cast-off can be made from the floppy disks. When you list the files on the disk, the system will tell you the amount of space used (or remaining, which amounts to the same thing). A standard, double-density 5 1/4" disk holds about 180,000 characters, so a simple calculation will convert the percentage of space taken up by the copy into a cast-off. Again, remember to subtract 1 percennt for format commands.

this hyphen will be typeset

watch out for typos – they will mess up your cast-off

If you are dealing with old-fashioned hard copy, pounded out on a typewriter, you have to do some old-fashioned $\frac{1}{M}$ but not particularly hard $\frac{1}{M}$ manual calculations.

dashes are single typset characters

The quick-and-dirty method, which should be used only with longer manuscripts, is to find the average length of the typewritten line by sampling several pages, and multiplying the result by the number of lines in the copy.

A more precise method involves several steps.

First, find the shortest full line on each page, ignoring

shortest line

ally a good idea anyway to delete word-break hyphens before you start the cast-off. Be careful, however, to leave compound-word hyphens (which will be typeset) that happen to fall at the end of a line.

The quickest, and safest, way to count characters is to make a character-gauge by typing a row of numerals along the edge

The Haber rule has gauges for typewritten copy, inches, and a variety of text face sizes. It simplifies copyfitting and marking proof for page or column breaks.

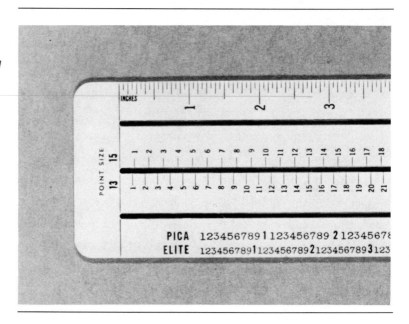

of a sheet of paper, being careful to use the same size of type as the manuscript copy.

Even better, buy yourself a Haber rule which has gauges for elite and pica type, as well as gauges for most common text-type sizes. It is an invaluable tool for the type designer, and costs only a few dollars.

One warning, however; this copyfitting method will not work for copy typed on a variable-spacing machine such as the IBM executive typewriters. In standard machines, the characters are equally spaced and align vertically, so that every cut-off line automatically has the same number of characters. There is no accurate method for counting variably-spaced copy—apart from counting every character individually—so you might as well use the average-line method.

Special settings, such as lists or indented quotations, must be cast-off separately, particularly if you plan to set them in a different face from the main text. Remember to include any additional linespacing above and below special settings. Similarly, you must allow for in-text heads, and your life will be simpler if you establish a fixed number of text lines per head.

Once you have the cast-off, you can plan your design pragmatically. You can, for instance, decide on an appropriate typeface for the text, although you may find you have to juggle your specifications later to fit the copy.

When you have settled on a typeface, it is relatively simple to compute the number of lines of type represented by the copy from the character-count tables in your type catalog or type specimen book.

There are several different styles of character-count tables, but the most common is a characters-per-pica scale like this:

TYPEFACE NAME	CHARACTER PER PICA										
	6	7	8	9	10	11	12	14	18	24	30
Perpetua Roman T/D	5.16	4.42	3.87	3.44	3.09	2.81	2.58	2.21	1.72	1.29	1.03
Perpetua Italic T/D	5.54	4.75	4.15	3.69	3.32	3.02	2.77	2.37	1.85	1.38	1.11

This is the scale for the text face of this book, 11 point Perpetua. The chart indicates that 11 point Perpetua sets at 2.81 characters per pica. On the specified 24 pica line, then, we will have an average of 68 characters (actually 67.44, but there is no such thing as a fraction of a character).

To find the number of type lines, all you have to do is to divide the cast-off total by the number of characters in a single line. If the division is not exact—and it rarely will be—round off any fraction to the next highest whole number.

Again, however, we have a problem. This method works perfectly for metal or phototypesetting systems. It will not work for digital systems, which usually have variable letter- and word-spacing parameters built in.

The character-count tables are based on averages taken from thousands of lines of typeset copy, set with conventional letter-spacing. If your type is to be set digitally, the tables will not be applicable unless you specify conventional spacing, and, even then, will still be inaccurate if the system is programmed for automatic kerning.

Digital type books often do not have character-count scales, which are almost meaningless when so many type parameters can be specified. They do, however, give alphabet lengths (which allow for automatic kerning), so, with some additional effort, you can arrive at a fairly satisfactory result. A formula for converting alphabet length with normal letterspacing is:

$$342/\text{alphabet length in points} = \text{characters per pica}$$

If you are using another letterspacing option, consult with your typesetter on the best way to calculate line-length.

It will probably be some time before we have the digital equivalents of the traditional tables because of the variations in the different systems. They may well take the form of computer programs. In the meantime, thank heavens for pocket calculators.

CALCULATING THE COPY BLOCK

The final step is to compute the vertical space, or depth, of the type. The formula is:

$$\text{depth of line} \times \text{number of lines} = \text{depth of type}$$

If your type is set solid, the depth of the line is the same as the type size; if you have linespaced, it is the type size plus the amount of linespacing. More simply, the line depth is the number after the slash in your type specification (11/13 Perpetua).

Once you know how much vertical space the type will take up, you can design your copy blocks to fit the copy comfortably. Obviously, you have to account for heads, special settings, and illustrations as well, but at least you have a fairly accurate idea of how much space to allow for the various elements.

ADJUSTING SPECIFICATIONS

At this stage, you may find your original specifications are unworkable. The type size or measure you selected may leave you with a text that is far too long or too short. With an accurate copyfit, however, you can adjust the specifications in a variety of ways without having to abandon your design plan entirely.

The most obvious solution would be to cut or add copy, but this is a luxury allowed to few designers. In most cases, once the text has been approved, it is cast in concrete.

That still leaves you with a number of palatable options.

If the text is short, you can specify a larger size of type. If it is long, you can scale down a size.

Similarly, you can switch to a looser- or tighter-setting face. Appendix C will give you some alternatives to start with.

You can also increase or decrease linespacing, or, if more drastic action is needed, shorten or increase the measure. (If the maximum measure for this book were increased to 25 picas, we would increase the number of characters per page by about 100, which is equivalent to 2 lines per page.)

Finally, you can increase or decrease the depth of the type block.

And, of course, you could combine any or all of these remedies.

The secret, of course, is that precise copyfitting allows you to make deliberate adjustments that will produce the results you want. You won't be shooting in the dark.

B TEXT FACES BY X-HEIGHT

Here are the text faces from Chapter 3 listed by family in increasing order of x-height. The effect of x-height is essentially optical, rather than mechanical, and obviously involves a number of other factors, which have not been considered here. The x-height comparisons are direct comparisons made by measuring the lower-case x's enlarged from 14 points to approximately 180 points. The numbers following the names of the faces then are an arbitrary index of size, useful only for a rough comparison.

OLD STYLES

Cloister 19.6
Perpetua 19.8
Granjon 21.5
Weiss 22.5
Goudy Old Style 22.9
Bembo 23.3
Electra 23.3
Garamond 23.4
Janson 24
Caslon 540 24.8
Times Roman 26

TRANSITIONALS

Fournier 22.9
Scotch Roman 23
Bulmer 23.1
Fairfield 24
Baskerville 24.5

MODERNS

Bodoni 21.4
Didot 22
Caledonia 23
De Vinne 23.8
Torino 26.3
Century Expanded 27
Walbaum 28
Craw Modern 29.3
Cooper Black 29.8

TWO-WEIGHT SQUARE SERIFS

Cheltenham 22.4
Bookman 25.5
Melior 25.8
Souvenir 26
Century Schoolbook 26.5
Clarendon 26.5

MONOWEIGHT SQUARE-SERIFS

Stymie 25.8
Memphis 26
Rockwell 27.5

UNEVEN-WIDTH SANS SERIFS

Kabel 22.4
Gill Sans 25
Futura 25.8

EVEN-WIDTH SANS SERIFS

Standard 25.8
Folio 26
Univers 27.8
Eurostile 28
News Gothic 28.8
Helvetica 29.8
Avant Garde 30
Franklin Gothic 30

SHADED SANS SERIFS

Peignot 22.5
Optima 26.5
Friz Quadrata 26.7
Eras 28
Ad Lib 28.3
Britannic 30

C TEXT FACES BY WIDTH

Here are the text faces from Chapter 3 listed by family in increasing order of set width, which was determined by measuring the 12 point lower-case alphabets, normally letterspaced. Bracketed faces have identical or almost identical measures.

OLD STYLES

Cloister
Perpetua
⎰Goudy Old Style
⎱Granjon
Weiss
Caslon 540
⎰Garamond
⎱Janson
⎰Bembo
⎱Electra
Times Roman
Palatino

TRANSITIONALS

Bulmer
Fournier
Fairfield
Scotch Roman
Baskerville

MODERNS

Torino
Didot
Bodoni
De Vinne
Caledonia
Craw Modern
Walbaum
Century Expanded
Cooper Black

TWO-WEIGHT SQUARE SERIFS

Cheltenham
Souvenir
Century Schoolbook
{Bookman
{Melior
Clarendon

MONOWEIGHT SQUARE SERIFS

Rockwell
{Stymie
{Beton
Memphis

UNEVEN-WIDTH SANS SERIFS

Gill Sans
Futura
Kabel

EVEN-WIDTH SANS SERIFS

News Gothic
Standard
Folio
{Helvetica
{Univers 55
Franklin Gothic
Avant Garde

SHADED SANS SERIFS

Peignot
{Eras
{Britannic
Optima
Friz Quadrata
Eurostile
Ad Lib

D BIBLIOGRAPHY

There is a vast literature on typography, graphic design, and printing technologies, much of which is highly technical. Most of it is not included here. This is simply a highly selective list of books that should be helpful to someone just finding his or her feet in the design craft.

It is sadly deficient in typography texts because designers seem oddly diffident about writing on the subject at a more basic level. Most type books are by experts for experts.

The texts listed here can generally be found in larger bookstores and graphic arts supply houses. Two must be ordered directly from the publisher and I have noted that in the comments. Generally they are fairly expensive items, but I have not given prices because they change quickly these days. However, I think that any of the books listed here is well worth the expense.

Craig, James. **_Designing With Type_** (Watson-Guptill)

TYPE AND TYPOGRAPHY

An excellent introductory text in a semi-worktext format, and perhaps the most popular for design courses. It is not as detailed as this book, but the larger trim size allows for more extensive illustration. There are some interesting and useful end-of-chapter exercises. Craig's later _Phototypesetting_ seems to me to be less useful. The content appears to be little more than a rehash of _Designing With Type_ and is not as well organized.

Gates, David. *Type* (Watson-Guptill)

A working designer's encyclopedia of typefaces, with over six hundred specimens, many in a variety of sizes. Unlike the conventional type encyclopedia, it is sensibly organized by type family, a far more useful arrangement for the practitioner.

Lee, Marshall. *Bookmaking* (R. R. Bowker)

Just about everything you could want to know about designing and editing books—but much more than that. Lee deals not only with the mechanics of typography, but also with the more elusive creative process of design in a thoughtful, practical and readable manner. My only criticism of the book is the stinginess of the illustrations.

Tschichold, Jan. *Treasury of Alphabets and Lettering* (Reinhold)

This translation of Tschichold's *Meisterbuch der Schrift* is a classic expert's book for experts, but I couldn't resist including it. The "text" is a collection of the author's favorite faces, elegantly displayed; it is an object-lesson in the art of display. The meat of the book, however, is the delightfully doctrinaire introduction, which deals with many of the refinements of type design. The translation is pedestrian, but it is worth slogging through if you want to learn some of the tricks of the trade from a master typographer.

LAYOUT AND DESIGN

Hurlbut, Alan. *Layout* (Van Nostrand)

A practical guide to the techniques of arranging type and illustration. Hurlbut has written several other books on the subject from a more theoretical standpoint; they might well be worth consulting at a later point.

Nelson, Roy Paul. *Publication Design* (William C. Brown)

A well-illustrated and knowledgeable handbook on the design of a wide variety of print formats, from newspapers to newsletters, flyers, and even student yearbooks. The examples are drawn not only from the glossier productions in each category, but also from the less ambitious publications.

——— *The Design of Advertising* (William C. Brown)

An uneven book in some respects, but it is sound on creative type display in its ultimate form, print advertising, and on what the author calls "long-term design"—logotypes, trade marks and the like.

White, Jan V. *Editing By Design* (R. R. Bowker)

Deceptively titled, this is a breezy dissertation on design by a leading magazine designer. Although ostensibly limited to magazines, it has much broader applications. There probably isn't a better discussion of the creative handling of artwork or a more intelligible discussion of grids anywhere. Abundantly—even, exuberantly—illustrated.

Craig, James. *Production for the Graphic Designer* (Watson-Guptill)

TECHNOLOGY AND MECHANICS

A compendium of information on the manufacturing processes, from typesetting to papermaking and binding, all lavishly illustrated. Its only drawback is that it has not yet caught up to the digital revolution, but that deficiency will presumably be corrected in future editions. In the meantime, it is an indispensible handbook.

Gates, David. *Graphic Design Studio Procedures* (Lloyd-Simone)

A detailed and very practical handbook on the preparation of copy for typesetting and printing. Also fully illustrated. It is the perfect complement to the preceding book.

International Paper Company. *Pocket Pal*

A miniature classic. *Pocket Pal* is a condensed version of *Production for the Graphic Designer*, and may be the best small handbook in any technical field. Order directly from IPC, but get your order in early for the next edition. Almost everyone else in the business will be after it.

Dean Lem Associates. ***Graphics Master***

A uniquely useful planning aid, containing just about everything a designer needs. It has a built-in proportion wheel, tables of standard paper weights and envelope sizes, showings of dozens of typefaces, and an encyclopedic set of character-count tables which give the varying characters-per-pica for the different manufacturers' versions of the different faces. Very expensive but almost indispensable. Order from Dean Lem Associates, P.O. Box 46086, Los Angeles CA 90046.

RELATED MATTER   ***Webster's New Collegiate Dictionary***

Why would a designer want this dictionary? First, to avoid that cardinal sin, a typographic error in a headline. Second, because this is the final authority on word-breaks and hyphenation, superseding Webster's 3. And finally, because, if you haven't a proper drawing table, it will give you the ideal working slope if you prop up a drawing board on it.

Skillin, M. E. and R. M. Gay. ***Words Into Type*** (Appleton)

A sound, if slightly conservative, handbook on editorial style—where to place punctuation correctly, how to capitalize and abbreviate, how to handle foreign languages, and so on. While not as encyclopedic as the "bible", the Chicago *Manual of Style*, it is far more practical from a designer's point of view.

PERIODICALS   Many of the periodicals in the field are highly specialized, highly technical, or highly esoteric. The one publication listed here, however, should be on every designer's reading list.

U & lc. Published quarterly by International Typographic Corporation.

Originally designed as a showpiece for ITC's new faces, this has become a showpiece for contemporary creative type design. And it is free to practitioners in the field. Order from ITC, 216 East 45th Street, New York NY 10017.

INDEX

Typefaces are listed under their original names in small caps; alternative names are italicized and cross-referenced to the original name. Illustrations are boldfaced.

A

accented characters, 36, **36**
accents, 36, **36**
AD LIB, 89
agate, 27
agate inches, 27
Airport. See Futura
Akzidenz Grotesk. See Standard
Alcuin of York, 6
Aldine Roman. See Bembo
Alexandria. See Stymie
alphabet, 3
   lower case, **35**, 36
   nonroman, 40, **40**
   readability of, 114
   upper case, **35**, 36
alphabet length, 111, 193, 199–200
Alpha Gothic. See NEWS GOTHIC,
Alphavers. See Univers
AMELIA, 93
AMERICAN ANTIQUE, 98
AMERICANA OUTLINE, 96
American-British point, 26
American Typefounders, 53, 71, 72
AMERICAN TYPEWRITER, 93
Andover. See Palatino
antique finish, 185
apex, **41**, 42
Aries. See Univers
arm, 41, **41**
ARNOLD BÖCKLIN, 98
ascender, **42**, 43
as patches, 50
ASTORIA, 95
AUGUSTEA, 94
AUGUSTEA SHADED, 97
Austin, Richard, 68, 98

author's alteration (AA), 160
AVANT GARDE, 85

B

Ballardvale. See Melior
BALLOON BOLD, 93
baseline, 42, **42**, 43
basis weight, 183, 184
Baskerline. See Baskerville
Baskerstar. See Baskerville
BASKERVILLE, 65
Baskerville, John, 66, 67, 98
Bauer, Konrad, 86
Bauhaus, 81, 82, 85
Baum, Walter, 86
Beaumont. See Baskerville
Bem. See Bembo
BEMBO, 62, 64
BEN FRANKLIN INITIALS, 100
Benton, Loyd, 71
Benton, Morris F., 62, 77, 78, 86, 87, 99
Besley, R. and Company, 74
BETON, 79
blade-coated finish, 186
blues, 51
BO. See Bodoni
BODONI, 68, 69
Bodoni, Giambattista, 68, 110
BODONI POSTER, 70
Bodonistar. See Bodoni
body (of type), 25
boldface, 36, **38**
   for emphasis, 145
   linespacing of, 123, **123**
   for minor heads, 142
   readability of, 115
Bookface. See Bookman

INDEX

INDEX

thick stroke, 41, **41**
thin space, 31, **31**
thin stroke, 41, **41**
THORNE SHADED, 97
thumbnail, 46, **47**, 107
THUNDERBIRD, 99
tight letterspacing, 117, **118**
Times New Roman. See Times Roman
TIMES ROMAN, 64, 94
Times Star. See Times Roman
titling family, 94ff
Toledo. See News Gothic
TORINO, 72
TR. See Times Roman
Trade Gothic. See News Gothic
Trajanic capitals, 94, 95
transfer type, 170
transitional family, 55ff
transparent design, 102
trim size, 52
Tschichold, Jan, 116, 124
Tuscan face, 99
Twentieth Century. See Futura
two-weight, 44, **44**
two-weight square serif family, 74ff
type size, 26
    nonstandard, 29, **29**
    standardized, 28, **28**
typewriter, 169
typographic family, 84ff

U

u and lc, 151–52
UN. See Univers
uncial, 5, **5**
uncoated stock, 184
uneven-width monoweight sans serif family, 82ff
Unistar. See Univers
unit system, 31–32, **32**
UNIVERS, 84
upper case, 25, **35**, 36
   readability of, 114, **115**
Uranus. See Melior

Ursa. See Optima
Utica. See Futura

V

Varityper, 169
Vega. See Helvetica
Venetian oldstyle, 58, 62, 64
Ventura. See Melior
Versatile. See Univers
vertical type, 147, **147**
very tight letterspacing, 117, 118
visual opacity, 184

W

WALBAUM, 72
Walbaum, Justin, 73
Waltham. See Microgramma
weight, 43, **43**, 44
WEISS, 65
Weiss, Emir Rudolf, 65
widow, 149–50
Winchester. See Cheltenham
Wolf, Rudolf, 79
wordspacing, 116, 120
   optimal display, 128–29, **128**
   optimal text, 117, 118, **119**, 120ff
writing paper, 183

X

x-height, **42**, 43
   comparative, 111, 197–98
   influence on readability, 109–10
x-line, 42, **42**

Z

Zapf, Herman, 64, 76, 88, 94, 110
ZAPF CHANCERY, 92
Zapf von Hesse, Gudrun, 98
Zenith. See Optima